CHILD CUSTODY

Practice Standards, Ethical Issues, And Legal Safeguards for Mental Health Professionals

Robert Henley Woody

Professional Resource Press
Sarasota, Florida

Published by Professional Resource Press
(An imprint of Professional Resource Exchange, Inc.)
Post Office Box 15560
Sarasota, FL 34277-1560

The copy editor for this book was Brian Fogarty, the typesetter was Denise Franck, the managing editor was Debra Fink, the production coordinator was Laurie Girsch, and Jami S. Stinnet created the cover.

Library of Congress Cataloging-in-Publication Data

Woody, Robert Henley.
   Child custody : practice standards, ethical issues, and legal
safeguards for mental health professionals / Robert Henley Woody.
      p. cm.
   Includes bibliographical references and index.
   ISBN 1-56887-062-0 (alk. paper)
      1. Custody of children--United States. 2. Psychology, Forensic--
United States. 3. Evidence, Expert--United States. I. Title.

KF505.5.Z9. W66 2000
346.7301'73--dc21
                                             00-023853

DEDICATION

This book is dedicated to my children, Matthew Levi Henley Woody, Robert Henley Woody, III, and Jennifer Kate Henley Woody, over whom their mother and I never had a custody dispute—except who had to keep them if one of us decided to run away for a life of fun, frivolity, and social irresponsibility!

TABLE OF CONTENTS

FOREWORD

As a psychologist in the 1960s, I was brought into child custody disputes by legal process. That is, I was essentially a psychodiagnostician and therapist, and attorneys for some of my clients sought my testimony—the attorneys and clients came to me, I did not go to them. By legal process, I had little choice but to participate in an area that was not a particular interest.

My Doctor of Philosophy degree program at Michigan State University and subsequent study at the University of London's Institute of Psychiatry and the Washington School of Psychiatry had provided me, I believe, with a solid knowledge of human behavior and clinical methods, and had inculcated a strong commitment to behavioral science, ethical conduct, and professional standards. To this day, I am unreserved in endorsing the scientist-practitioner approach to mental health services. Nonetheless, like most of my psychologist-peers at the time, I entered into child custody proceedings with little knowledge about legal processes in general and child custody testimony in specific.

It was an era when our society was wrapping up the "social revolution," which can be described aptly as conflict oriented. The penchant for volatile "in your face" encounters permeated child custody cases.

In part because of the redefinition of gender roles, as spawned by the feminist movement, more divorcing fathers began to seek custody of their children. When the parents could not agree on residential custody or visitation, the matter was submitted to the court. More often than not, these courtroom proceedings revealed a no-holds-barred competition between the parents, commonly with open hostility. Needless to say, the animosity cast a long-term pall on postdivorce parental relations, subjecting the children to risk of detrimental parenting.

It was an age when the questions were being posed about whether the best interests of the child justified deference to the natural parents, as opposed to psychological parents. For example, grandparents with a history of protecting and caring for the children more than the natural parents sought custody.

The animus that pervaded the child custody legal proceedings became part of the popular culture, as evidenced in the movie *Kramer Versus Kramer* (Jaffe & Benton, 1979). In the mass media, accounts of controversial custody decisions abounded. Legislation was passed and judicial decisions were rendered that made the courtroom ripe for parental conflicts. Even I wrote a book for popular consumption titled *Getting Custody: Winning the Last Battle of the Marital War* (Woody, 1978), which admittedly did little or nothing to resolve the negatives associated with child custody disputes.

Among other things, my aforementioned book led to my receiving nationwide requests to provide expert testimony. I plunged ahead, trying to construct an academic and practice model that would have a reasonable behavioral science basis. In retrospect, I suspect there were faults, but I tried to the best of my ability.

Society's embrace of the conflict model for child custody cases resulted in the legal proceedings becoming rife with mental health practitioners offering opinions about all sorts of elements in postdivorce relations, ostensibly in service to the best interests of the child. The term "hired gun" became part of the child custody lexicon.

Supported by public policy, many experts all too often stated opinions about legal issues, including which parent should be awarded custodial rights, that relied on little or no scholarship or professional knowledge base. In other words, mental health professionals lacked behavioral science information about how to objectively and reasonably assess factors in that area critical to child custody determinations, yet made proclamations about what factors would be in the best interests of the children and how each of the parents measured up.

By answering the ultimate legal questions in the proceedings, namely which parent should receive primary residential custody and what should be the visitation schedule for the noncustodial parent, the self-ordained "experts," notwithstanding their lack of research or training for the decision making, became quasi-judges or pseudo triers of fact. For many, it was a heady experience.

Admittedly, I was bothered by what I and others like me were being asked to do in the name of professionalism. Thanks to a postdoctoral grant from the U.S. Office of Education, I was able to pursue full-time study at the University of Pittsburgh's Graduate School of Public Health. My dissertation for the Doctor of Science degree was on the criteria for child custody legal proceedings used by lawyers, psychiatrists, psychologists, and social workers (Woody, 1975). The results of my research will be discussed later. This postdoctoral study and research led to a lasting commitment to improving the involvement of mental health professionals in child custody cases, be it as an evaluator, therapist, mediator, or expert critiquing the work of other professionals.

Along the line, I became a devotee of healthy family relations and infatuated with pursuit of excellence in the law (I probably saw the movie *The Paper Chase* [Thompson et al., 1973] one too many times). I augmented my training in education, psychology, and health services with a Juris Doctor degree from Creighton University's School of Law. Upon becoming an attorney, my work in forensic psychology took a dramatic shift: I became legal counsel for mental health practitioners for, among other things, their involvement in child custody cases.

To date, I have assisted, literally, several hundred mental health professionals (representing medicine, marriage and family therapy, mental health counseling, nursing, psychology, and social work) about countless issues and practices relevant to child custody cases. I have learned a lot!

In providing professional services for child custody cases, it is clear that the mental health practitioner, regardless of competency and experience, faces a high risk of ethical, regulatory (licensing), and legal (malpractice) complaints. Moreover, the current efforts for consumer protection against allegedly errant mental health practitioners, often marred by overly zealous attitudes and practices by the investigators, monitors, regulators, and decision makers, essentially create a playing field that is tilted to the advantage of the complainant. This prosecutorial approach jeopardizes the mental health practitioner's right of being presumed innocent until proven guilty and having due process under the law (Woody, 1993).

At a national conference of a major mental health professional association, the chair of its ethics committee declared to the audience: "If you want an ethics complaint, work in child custody" (Stricker, 1998). Because of the zealous "consumer protection" system that pervades contemporary complaint situations, the risk of a complaint is great and the disadvantage experienced by the mental health practitioner is profound. I have witnessed innumerable practitioners retreating from forensic work in general, and being particularly negative about working with a child custody dispute. Relatedly, the punitive "guilty until proven innocent" framework that surrounds the processing of ethical, regulatory, and legal complaints has resulted in, I believe, injustices being imposed on some mental health practitioners. The outcome is, of course, harmful consequences to professional careers, and well-qualified practitioners making themselves unavailable to child custody proceedings. With the travesties of justice that occur in this scenario, there are negative effects for all concerned, including our society.

The best protection for the interests of children, parents, professionals, and our society comes from well-defined and scholarly based ethics, laws, standards, and guidelines. The contents of this book and my ideas and suggestions are intended to promote conceptualizations and practices that will benefit children, families, professionalism, and society alike. Participation of mental health professionals, such as in offering testimony to the court, should be founded on academic and empirical information, solid education and training, sound logic and reasoning, and objectivity, and should be free from personal prejudice and bias, undue subjectivity, and self-aggrandizing advocacy. This recommendation sets the stage for the contents of this book.

Some mental health practitioners will question or oppose certain of my guidelines. That is, I knowingly offer guidelines that are not supported by all mental health practitioners. The reason is simple: I offer the guidelines both to enhance the quality of the professional services and to offer legal safeguards to the mental health practitioner. From analysis of complaint cases, I am aware of alternatives to many of the guidelines that I set forth (e.g., relevant to answering the ultimate legal questions), but I am also aware of the views and conduct on the part of the mental health practitioner that lead to complaints. In an effort to stay complaints, sometimes prudent and conservative choices are necessary.

It should be noted that the contents of this book may seemingly be geared more to psychologists than to the practitioners in the other mental health disciplines. That notion is understandable, but untrue. As compared to marriage and family therapy, mental health counseling, medicine (including psychiatry), nursing, and social work, psychology has given the most emphasis to specific professional ethics and standards relevant to forensic services and child custody cases. Also, my identity as a mental health professional is primarily aligned with psychology, although I have worked as an attorney and professor with practitioners from all of the professional disciplines. There is considerable material from psychology, which is used in an exemplary manner, and is applicable to every mental health discipline.

This book is intended to inform a wide array of persons about child custody cases, particularly the testimony that will be provided by mental health practitioners. The contents aim to be useful to all mental health practitioners, regardless of the professional discipline. In addition to self-study, the book will be useful for graduate-level courses that focus on child and family interventions, and ethical and legal aspects of professional practice. I have structured the book to cover the core areas deemed essential by professional ethics and standards, including child development, family relations and systems (e.g., parenting, psychopathology, dysfunction, and abuse), role(s) and functions, specialized intervention and assessment strategies, and ethical and legal aspects of child custody. The book is structured, therefore, to constitute a comprehensive mini-course for the topic of child custody, as might assist a mental health practitioner to acquire the knowledge and skills necessary to work in the area.

The contents of the book will help attorneys understand the appropriate and inappropriate use of testimony by mental health practitioners. Thus, attorneys will be able to elicit and insist on proper performance by those who provide testimony.

For the person who is in the midst of, or coping with, post-divorce custody matters, this book will clarify what occurs in child custody legal proceedings. Also, parents will learn what to expect of the mental health practitioners who provide treatment, evaluation, mediation, or expert testimony.

Despite my concern about the escalation of complaints against mental health practitioners, the material herein will provide attorneys and their clients with an understanding of accepted views and conduct on the part of a mental health practitioner. Stated differently, the guidelines help clarify what should and should not be done by a mental health practitioner involved in testifying in child custody cases. Therefore, the attorneys and their clients can identify seeming transgressions and seek appropriate sanctions against the allegedly errant mental health practitioner.

Finally, it is important to state that any comments about the law should be tempered with the fact that each jurisdiction has its unique laws and rules for the matters discussed herein. Throughout the book, I have made repeated comments about the possible legal differences between jurisdictions. If there is any doubt or question, the mental health practitioner should seek counsel from an attorney qualified to practice in the jurisdiction at issue.

Chapter 1

UNDERSTANDING THE EFFECTS
OF DIVORCE

Today, children face perilous conditions, which must be counteracted by society. Since children represent the human resources for the future of our society, any jeopardy to children also means jeopardy to our society. Consider the following caution:

> Children are our hope for the future. They need and deserve consistent love, support and nurturing from both parents, whether their parents live in the same home with them or not. The family is the critical learning center where children are taught the virtues of responsibility and concern for others by the examples set by their parents. However, the examples set by some parents are less than virtuous. (Engler & Quinn, 1998, p. 276)

This proclamation establishes a primary message for this book, namely the essence of our society depends upon both parents' providing a child with a healthy family.

➡ *Guideline:* The mental health practitioner has a responsibility to promote the best interests of children for purposes of protecting the human resources of society.

Unfortunately, lawmakers and mental health practitioners alike have failed to adequately protect children. By definition, lawmakers have the duty to create a governmental system that will enable mental health practitioners to promote effective parenting and family life, and help the less-than-virtuous parents improve the relationships with their children and each other. As will be evident, there is presently a collision course between public policy, government, and mental health services, as revealed by the elevated risk of ethical, regulatory (licensing), and legal (malpractice) complaints relevant to children's services in general and child custody matters in particular.

THE THREAT FROM DIVORCE

Divorce is exposing children to adverse conditions (Wallerstein, 1994). In today's American society, approximately one-half of all marriages end in divorce (Bogolub, 1995). The result is that most children do not live in the stereotyped two-parent family. Looking at the year 1993, Dickson (1995) summarizes data from the United States Census Bureau:

> In the same year, out of 64.2 million children, 46.6 million lived with two parents, 15.5 million lived only with their mothers and 2.2 million lived only with their fathers. Between 1970 and 1990, the percentage of children living in two-parent homes declined from 85 percent to 73 percent. Looking at the data another way, female-headed households with children grew from 10 percent to 20 percent over the same period, male-headed households with children grew from 1 percent to 4 percent, and two-parent households with children decreased from 89 percent to 76 percent. (pp. 247-248)

Noting that the complexity of the family has changed, Dickson reveals that, in 1990, nearly one-quarter of all married-couple families with children were nontraditional: "Seventy-seven percent of 25.3 million married-couple families consisted of parents and their biological or adoptive children; 10 percent consisted of mothers, their children, and a stepfather; less that 1 percent consisted of fathers, their children, and a stepmother; and 11 percent consisted of parents and stepparents, with biological and adoptive children of both parents" (p. 248).

To increase the risks associated with divorce, our society presents children and their families with detrimental living conditions. Brooks-Gunn and Duncan (1998) note that about 20 percent of American children are in families with an income below the threshold of poverty. Viewed differently, children constitute 40 percent of persons living in poverty. From their review of the research and analysis of policy and practice, they conclude that well-being is impacted by poverty: "The effects are most pronounced for children who are very poor, persistently poor, or poor during their first five years of life" (p. 18). The poverty issue becomes of particular concern when it is recognized that many divorced parents may not be able or do not provide adequate financial support for their children: "The lack of financial support has a devastating emotional impact on these children, and also has a significant impact on the financial status of the custodial family and the community the family resides in" (Engler & Quinn, 1998, p. 276).

➜ *Guideline: The mental health practitioner should be capable of conceptualizing the "family" in nontraditional terms.*

The turmoil and negative conditions associated with divorce have the potential to harm parents and children alike, as well as impact negatively on the extended family and, in fact, society as a whole. Unless counteracted, the adverse effects of divorce will reduce our nation's human resources. For example, stress associated with divorce can create health problems and reduce the parent's effectiveness in work and other interpersonal relationships and the child's learning and social-emotional behavior. Also, the negative consequences on the persons experiencing divorce can erode the moral fiber of our society. Many folks believe that divorce has already produced horrible erosion, and the matter has reached a crisis point.

On a positive note, Bogolub (1995) does not deny the potential of adverse effects on children and youth from divorce, but believes that it takes "its toll on children—but generally on a temporary basis" (p. 15), and suggests that "most children are not severely harmed by divorce" (p. 19). Given certain contradictory research studies (e.g., Wallerstein, 1984, 1994), Bogolub's positivism may or may not be correct. Certain trends, however, offer hope that children will survive the potential negative effects of divorce (e.g., increased acceptance of divorce within our society, legislative and case law that support both parents having continued postdivorce involvement in the lives of their children, and an apparent decline in litigiousness between divorcing parents). Although the latter is still a weak trend, it seems to be furthered by legislative and judicial actions that encourage or require that divorcing parents receive education or mediation about custody and visitation. The destructive tide will be turned only by effort from all concerned, such as increased efforts by mental health practitioners (as well as educators and others) to help the children of divorce develop in a healthy fashion.

Recognizing the potential for harmful effects from divorce, the executive branch of our government has formulated national policies directed at promoting so-called "family values." In turn, the legislative and judicial branches have created legal means for counteracting the negative consequences of divorce. Accordingly, mental health professionals now have a considerable role in legal proceedings directed at custody, visitation, and abuse issues (note: in this book, the term "custody" is used in the generic, embodying a range of child-related issues that emerge when parents divorce). Regrettably, neither national policies nor laws have given adequate importance to establishing, funding, and maintaining community mental health services, especially important for citizens who are socially and economically disenfranchised. (See Brooks-Gunn and Duncan [1998] for frightening information about how poverty impacts the well-being of children and youth.)

This book is devoted to understanding the legal principles, judicial system, and professional concepts (which combined constitute a "psycholegal" framework) that are critical to a mental health practitioner's ability to adequately and appropriately serve the needs of individuals, family, and society in custody-related matters. Special attention is given to ethics, laws, standards, and guidelines that will improve the quality of services provided by mental health practitioners. As will be revealed, being involved in custody cases carries, unfortunately, a high risk of consumer dissatisfaction that will result in ethical, regulatory (licensing), and legal (malpractice) complaints. Therefore, the scope of this book is three-fold, namely helping the mental health practitioner (of any discipline): (a) acquire scholarly knowledge and conceptualizations relevant to child custody cases; (b) improve the quality of services provided to children, families, and courts; and (c) develop practice skills that will reduce risks and safeguard against ethical, regulatory, and legal complaints.

Further, although focused on mental health practitioners, the material should be informative to persons who are grappling with divorce-related matters. For example, parents who must deal with the effects of divorce will learn how the child custody cases are handled by the court, and what to expect of mental health practitioners who offer treatment, evaluation, mediation, or expert services. Also, their attorneys will gain insight into proper use of mental health practitioners relevant to treatment, evaluation, mediation, and expert testimony.

SOCIAL RESPONSIBILITY TO THE FAMILY SYSTEM

Becoming a mental health practitioner carries a social responsibility to benefit all service recipients (also known as clients, patients, or consumers). Most directly, this means helping the individual cope with personal problems, which commonly involve others, and learn new ways to perceive situations that are encountered. The social responsibility, however, goes even further; the mental health practitioner should be cognizant of the welfare and development of society in general. Consequently, mental health services must promote conditions within the individual and the immediate family (e.g., the "micro" level) that will afford constructive interactions with the array of interpersonal and interorganizational sources with whom there are connections (e.g., the "macro" level).

→ *Guideline: The mental health practitioner should deal with social systems at both the micro and macro levels.*

No system portends to impact the individual and society more than the family. The family constellation is composed of all those who have an explicit or implicit influence on the particular individual by blood or legal ties and, consequently, determine the amount of human resources that will be available to the individual. For children and youth, the linkages within the family may be: direct, such as those living in the same household or having frequent contact and intense emotional communications; or indirect, such as those who live elsewhere but have infrequent contacts, yet have occasional, perhaps less intense, emotional communications.

Those persons who constitute the so-called "immediate" family make up a "primary" group. That is, each member has the potential to have an impact on, and be impacted on in return by, every immediate family member. Although the potential for familial impact in general is strong, the members of even a primary group will vary in their influence or shaping power; and at some point, the interpersonal relationship will become distant enough figuratively and literally, to move beyond the primary group into the realm of a "secondary" group. For example, given our mobile society, aunts, uncles, and cousins who move away from what was once a close-knit family in the "home town" commonly have less influence as the years pass by. Perhaps for romantic love, the old adage "distance makes the heart grow fonder" is true, but for family relations, distance usually lessens the power to influence.

At various times during an individual's life, the members of his or her primary or secondary groups can move closer or further away, both geographically and psychologically. That is, there is the possibility that a member of a primary group will lose influence, but still remain in the individual's secondary groupings, and vice versa. As an example, a harping grandparent may eventually be perceived as a detrimental force and be rejected, with less frequent contacts and less communicative power; whereas a once-minimal friendship may yield enough positive communications to gain in influence.

An individual may be attracted to and/or alter the influence of another person, an interpersonal relationship, or an affiliation with an organization for either healthful or unhealthful reasons. Therefore, the mental health practitioner must always monitor relationships for positive effects; that is, an appropriate objective for therapeutic interventions is to lessen the power or preferably eliminate sources of negative influence.

→ *Guideline: When serving an individual or family, the mental health practitioner should analyze the influence emanating from primary and secondary group members, recognizing that this influence can change because of, for example, distance, interactive qualities, and competing forces.*

Chapter 2

CONSTRUCTING A THEORETICAL FRAMEWORK

Mental health services are conceptualized as the scientific study and modification of human behavior. In order to assess and intervene, the mental health practitioner must provide services within a theoretical framework that has been validated by behavioral science and is endorsed by a substantial sector of the profession. Consequently, the practitioner must be able to: define human behavior into classes or categories; operate by a regular method, which is orderly and consistent in procedure; and collect and analyze information about the individual and his or her relationships (Ford & Urban, 1998). In child custody, visitation, and abuse proceedings, no professional service should occur without this sort of scholarly and behavioral science foundation.

➜ *Guideline: The mental health practitioner should only provide services that have a reasonable scholarly and behavioral science foundation.*

The analysis is the method for formulation of the culminating "product," which enables professional judgments and opinions. Since the mental health practitioner relies on information that is plagued by subjectivity, the inferential process that underlies professional judgments and opinions creates a perilous pathway. As will be emphasized throughout this book, professional involvement in custody proceedings carries high risk of ethical, regulatory, and/or legal complaints.

Because of the inherent subjectivity of mental health analyses for assessment and interventions, as well as the concomitant judgments and opinions, the prudent mental health professional should constantly seek to maximize objectivity. For custody-related proceedings, objectivity is best gained by adopting an empirically based rationale for interpreting information, documenting the information in detail, and adhering to a nonadvocacy role. These issues will be discussed in greater detail later on.

Among mental health practitioners, there is no uniform agreement on the adequacy of any theoretical framework. Since therapeutic interventions (broadly defined) are so highly idiosyncratic to the needs of the client and the preferences and competencies of the therapist, there may be as many theoretical frameworks as there are practitioners. Even when certain qualifying criteria are applied, there is a mind-boggling conglomeration of so-called therapies. For example, Goldfried (1980) identified 130 approaches and Corsini (1981) thought there were as many as 250 approaches.

Before engaging in custody work, the mental health practitioner needs to establish an acceptable theoretical framework and staunchly maintain it in all professional services. To create a theoretical intervention framework, Robertson and Woody (1997) believe there are six dimensions that should be considered and accommodated: "(1) conscious versus unconscious determinants of behavior; (2) insight versus behavior change as the therapeutic goal; (3) a focus on the present-future versus the past; (4) a scientific versus aesthetic attitude; (5) the therapeutic relationship versus the therapist's techniques as a basis for change; and (6) diagnosis versus assessment" (p. 161). The framework should allow for services to pass through at least three stages:

> The first stage is developing a collaborative relationship, specifying problems, and prioritizing goals. The second stage consists of the therapist's application of specific interventions to implement therapeutic goals. The third stage is designed to generalize and maintain therapeutic gains. (p. 159)

Proactively, the mental health practitioner should construct a theoretical framework based on behavioral science and professionalism, thereby benefiting the client(s) with quality care and the practitioner with safeguards from complaints.

➔ *Guideline: The mental health practitioner should have a clear theoretical framework for all professional services.*

THEORETICAL CONSIDERATIONS

In this day and age, there are innumerable castigations of prominent theoretical approaches, namely because of the lack of empirical research to document efficacy. It is ill-advised to throw the baby out with the bathwater, and shy away from involvement in custody proceedings because one's theoretical framework will be scrutinized, questioned, and possibly "impeached" (e.g., one or more of the attorneys in the case will try to establish that the mental health practitioner's opinions lack credibility).

Selection of a theoretical framework for custody cases should be determined by the legal criteria for professional testimony and the existing research-related acceptance by members of the profession. At one time, legal proceedings seemed to favor psychoanalytic ideas, probably because of their historical prominence and longevity. In legal proceedings, any approach considered "humanistic" was and is still usually accorded dubious acceptance, which results in, for example, expert testimony based on humanistic theories receiving little weight in the decision making by the trier of fact (the judge or jury).

Nowadays, public policy, legal, and professional mental health sources seem to prefer that forensic roles draw on a blend of two theoretical approaches. One approach is cognitive social-learning, and the other is family systems.

According to the cognitive social-learning approach, an understanding of human behavior is defined primarily by the person's cognitions or thought processes. For example, when determining the applicability of mental status to a crime, the legal analysis focuses on the defendant's capacity for rational thought (Hermann, 1997).

According to the family systems approach, a person's behavior is not individually determined for causality and change. Just as there are many theoretical approaches to psychological assessment therapy in general, there are numerous ideas about family systems. In general, however, practitioners applying family systems theory "see a family not merely as a collection of individuals but as a whole that is greater than the sum of its parts" (Worden, 1999, p. 3).

The melding of cognitive social-learning and family systems is especially appropriate for the services provided by mental health practitioners relevant to child custody cases. Stated as a simple principle: Social reinforcements from the child's postdivorce family system will, along with certain biological/hereditary factors, produce the beliefs, attitudes, and conduct of the child.

The professional offering testimony in child custody cases should consider the foregoing principle. In other words, after interpreting the information and data, the mental health practitioner should formulate interpretations and opinions, which will be stated in testimony, that pass through a cognitive social-learning and family systems filter.

➡ **Guideline:** *Given the contemporary preferences of public policy, legal, and professional mental health sources, the mental health practitioner should accommodate the tenets of cognitive social-learning and family systems theories.*

THE COGNITIVE SOCIAL-LEARNING APPROACH

Given the preferences that prevail in public policy, law, and the mental health professions, the mental health practitioner should consider the relevance of a cognitive social-learning approach to the child custody matter at hand. When adopting this approach, the mental health practitioner need not forsake allegiance to certain other theoretical concepts.

It has long been recognized that behaviorally oriented approaches, such as cognitive social-learning, allow for integration of a variety of theoretical concepts and techniques (Lazarus, 1981, 1989; Woody, 1971). In other words, eclectic practice is defined by Brammer, Shostrom, and Abrego (1989) as "selecting concepts, methods, and strategies from a variety of current theories which work" (p. 11). Similarly, integration (a more recent term with more conceptual breadth than eclecticism) is characterized by Arkowitz (1992) as being open to "various ways of integrating diverse theories and techniques" (p. 262). Integration reflects: "Thoughtfully combining, blending, or distilling the best that the field had to offer, as gleaned from the literature, informal exchanges, and cumulative results of clinical experience" (Robertson & Woody, 1997, p. 190). The integrative approach seems to reflect the modern trend (Norcross & Goldfried, 1992). As Robertson (1995) puts it: "In the 1990s, eclecticism enjoys greater visibility and support than it has ever had before, and polemics between critics and apologists have all but disappeared" (p. 5).

→ *Guideline: When working in child custody cases, the mental health practitioner should avoid commitment to a singular theoretical approach (and certainly guard against any apostolic zeal in asserting theoretical notions), and seek to integrate theories that are relevant to the persons and situations at hand.*

At this point in time, there is reason to believe that testimony by mental health practitioners in child custody legal proceedings can best be formulated according to an integration of the cognitive social-learning and family systems approaches. This reliance on and melding of these two approaches will be discussed further in the remainder of this chapter, and in other chapters as well.

Throughout this book on child custody, ideas about the sort of judgments, opinions, and testimony expressed by the mental health professional will be relevant to a cognitive social-learning explanation for personality development, be it for the individual or for dynamics that occur in the context of primary and secondary groups.

The cognitive social-learning approach can and should be distinguished from behaviorism per se. The underlying notion of behaviorism is that "all behavior is ultimately contingency shaped, but an important subset of behavior is said to be rule governed," with a rule being "a verbal contingency-specifying stimulus" (Hayes, 1987, p. 332). The cognitive social-learning approach is not "restricted to a mindless listing of the links between particular cognitions and particular stimulus situations"; rather, consideration is given to "how these links go together into larger functional units relevant to the main enterprises of life" (Maddi, 1996, p. 451). Donovan and Chaney (1985) identify five intrapersonal variables that influence behavior in a specific situation:

> (1) cognitive and behavioral construction competencies, or what the person knows and can do; (2) encoding strategies and personal constructs, or how the individual appraises his or her world, and his or her characteristic ways of attributing responsibility for behavior; (3) cognitive expectancies or beliefs the individual holds about the outcome of his or her behavior or about his or her ability to execute a

given behavior; (4) subjective values or preferences, or what is particularly reinforcing for the person; and (5) self-regulatory systems and plans, or the methods utilized to maintain goal-directed behavior even in the absence of external support. (p. 353)

In regard to the assertion that the theoretical framework should be acceptable to the legal arena and supported by a substantial portion of the profession, the cognitive social-learning approach seems to be the contemporary approach of choice, along with (as will be explained in the next section) the family systems approach. Preference for the cognitive social-learning approach comes from its established research basis, which offers the distinct advantage of strengthening judgments, opinions, and testimony, as well as warding off complaints.

Although the cognitive social-learning approach allows for integration of ideas from other approaches, adaptations should be done rationally and cautiously to be sure that the effectiveness of the cognitive social-learning model, as established by research, is not diluted or lessened. Family systems concepts, which offer a broad theoretical framework, fit well with the cognitive social-learning model.

THE FAMILY SYSTEMS APPROACH

Given the purpose of professional services to child custody cases, the mental health practitioner must go beyond simply addressing factors, needs, or qualities associated with an individual or the dyad (involving the child and each of the parents). Rather, the public policy, legislative, and judicial intentions aim for a strong (or stronger) family unit subsequent to the divorce, notwithstanding the custody-visitation arrangements. Indeed, I have heard judges, licensing board and ethic committee members, and professional association leaders state emphatically, "From what we now know about child development, it is malpractice for any mental health professional to not deal with the entire family in child custody testimony." More will be said about this viewpoint later, such as how it is reflected in contemporary ethics, laws, and standards.

The reason for dealing with the entire family in any matter involving children, including in child custody cases, is simple. Although the parents will not be living together, each parent will continue to have an impact on the child throughout the child's life span. For example, even the absence, by abandonment or death, of a parent will have a continuing influence on the child. Also, the interactions between the divorced parents and between other family members will indirectly or directly affect the child.

→ **Guideline:** *The mental health practitioner should consider the postdivorce family system in which the child will (probably) live, and provide testimony that will address the nature of the anticipated family interactions and influences and offer opinions and information that are intended to foster family system benefits for all concerned.*

The cognitive social-learning approach for explaining and modifying human behavior is consonant with family systems theory. Recall the previously stated principle: Social reinforcements from the child's postdivorce family system will, along with certain biological/hereditary factors, produce the beliefs, attitudes, and conduct of the child.

Rather than a singular notion about a person's psychological conflicts or reinforcement contingencies causing specific behaviors, such as a "symptom" in a child, the family systems approach adopts an epistemology that:

- Decreases emphasis on individual motivation and increases emphasis on the effects of familial interactions;
- Dismisses lineal reasoning about causality (i.e., cause-and-effect relationships) and gives favor to circular causality (i.e., a family member's behavior affects others in the family, which responds with interactional effects that produce circular feedback loops to the individual and affects his or her behavior); and
- Minimizes the content of communications (i.e., what is said in a session) and maximizes the processes of communication (i.e., how the family as a whole and combinations of family members, particularly triads, verbally and nonverbally respond to issues and problems).

It is worthy of mention that, in yesteryears, these concepts were rarely dealt with in many professional mental health training programs. Since this stance has critical importance for contemporary child custody testimony, the mental health practitioner should make a special effort to obtain training in family systems, and since considerable research on family systems is emerging, staying abreast of the times requires an ongoing commitment by the mental health practitioner.

Of special benefit to working with a family embroiled in a child custody dispute, the family systems approach takes the onus off of blaming. No one alone, including a person with problems or symptoms that disrupt the family, is responsible or to blame for the negative conditions in the pre- or postdivorce family system. This stance obviously contradicts the posture adopted by certain attorneys, such as asserting: "My client is the victim of the other spouse's wrongful conduct and deserves to prevail on the legal issues before this honorable court."

Family systems work also encompasses a narrative perspective:

> From the narrative perspective, the psyche is not a fixed, objective entity but rather a fluid social construct or story that is subject to revision. The therapist's job is to help people "re-author" their stories, or elements of their stories, that are not serving them well. (Brock & Barnard, 1999, p. 8)

Therefore, the mental health practitioner "does not look for flaws but rather helps people to spot omissions in their story" (p. 8), particularly through questioning (which enriches and accelerates both assessment and therapy).

The family systems perspective externalizes the problem. That is, it "Encourages persons to objectify and, at times, to personify the problems that they experience as oppressive . . . [but] the problem becomes a separate entity and thus external to the person or relationship that was ascribed as the problem" (White & Epstein, 1990, p. 38).

Later on, there will be a more detailed discussion of the applicability of the cognitive social-learning and family systems approaches, individually and when integrated, for assessment and intervention purposes in child custody cases. At this point, it is useful to focus on the relevance of these two theoretical approaches to child custody testimony. As will be clear, there are considerations that will facilitate the mental health practitioner's efforts, but there will also be special challenges that will have to be met.

The adversarial nature of a child custody proceeding will result in two distinct presses. First, the mental health practitioner will be encouraged (by some attorneys and parents) to produce testimony that places blame on someone. Second, because of tradition and history, there will be efforts by attorneys, judges, and opposing experts to press the mental health practitioner to testify about diagnostic issues in a cause-and-effect manner, notwithstanding the fact that all concerned recognize this is not appropriate according to cognitive social-learning and family systems information. The evolution of the behavioral science for understanding human behavior contradicts testimony that embraces blame and linear causality.

➜ *Guideline: To deal with the challenges created by the adversarial nature of the child custody legal proceedings, the mental health practitioner should be up to date and well versed about relevant scholarly and behavioral science research that undergirds the testimony, and prepared to educate (i.e., respectfully refute or contradict) those who press for testimony that lacks a professional theoretical base.*

At opening the first chapter, the first guideline presented the idea of the best interests of the child. The revered "best interests of child" test, which will be explained in detail later, offers strong support for use of the cognitive social-learning and family systems approaches. Since the long-term objective is for the child to live and develop in a nurturing and healthy family, the influences from parental, sibling, intergenerational, and significant other sources should not be placed in a position of shame or blame, defensiveness, estrangement, or pathology. What is needed is a life span developmental objective for the child. Meeting the best interests of the child should be of concern for years to come, not just immediately after the child custody determination is made.

➜ *Guideline: The mental health practitioner should promote a life span developmental objective for the best interests of the child by de-emphasizing (or at least not solely or primarily relying on) the negatives that might emanate from a particular person or situation (i.e., avoid blaming), and specifying the persons and conditions that will contribute to the optimum positive development of the child for the long term.*

The foregoing ideas about concern for the child's best interests for years to come and the criteria specified (usually by statute) about what the mental health practitioner should consider and testify about combine to fashion a mandate for a multifactored assessment of each source (or as many sources as are feasible under the circumstances) that will be part of the child's foreseeable postdivorce family system. In addition to supporting the cognitive social-learning and family systems approaches, there is a mandate to complete a comprehensive evaluation and structure testimony accordingly.

➜ *Guideline: Since the health and well-being of the child should be safeguarded over his or her life span, not just in the immediate future, and the best interests of the child test sets forth multiple criteria for assessment and testimony, the mental health practitioner should strive to provide a revealing picture of the social-reinforcements that will occur or can be cultivated in the child's family system, and offer testimony that emphasizes individual and collective strengths.*

Certainly, this positive framework replaces the antiquated notion of declaring one of the parents to be "unfit" (and, in effect, awarding custody of the child to the parent who was "least unfit"). The negatives in the child's life can best be addressed and eliminated by formulating postdivorce conditions that will accentuate the positive.

Chapter 3

PROTECTING THE CHILDREN

Society recognizes that children are not fully competent to fend for themselves. Because of their young age, children are unable to make self determinations and implement personal safeguards. As discussed in Chapter 1, children are, of course, priceless human resources, and the future of society itself depends on maximizing their development:

> Children are presumed in law to be incomplete beings during the whole period of their development. Their inability to provide for their own basic needs, or even to maintain life without extraneous help, justifies their being automatically assigned at birth to their biological parents or, where this relationship either does not develop or fails to function, assigned by later court proceedings to parent substitutes. The intimate group of adults and their children constitute the central core of a family. Responsibility for the child— for her survival, for her physical and mental growth, and for eventual adaptation to community standards—thus becomes that of the designated adults or adult in a family to whom the child in turn is responsible and accountable. (J. Goldstein et al., 1996, p. 8)

By entering into the custody case, the mental health practitioner accepts a social responsibility for the well-being of children and youth. Moreover, as evidenced by the child's custody and care being under the auspices of the court, the parents and the mental health practitioner have a legal duty to protect the best interests of the child.

→ **Guideline:** *As relevant to "who is the client," the mental health practitioner's primary allegiance is to safeguarding the best interests of the child (e.g., regardless of who requests or pays for the services), recognizing that professional practice is both a social responsibility (established by professional ethics and standards) and a legal duty (which defines both role and function for involvement in the child custody case).*

Historically, children were treated as property or chattel of the parents, notably of the father. Only males could own property, and when it came to children, there was the legal duty placed on the father to protect, control, and financially support his children: "This absolute control stemmed from ancient Rome, where a father could sell his children or condemn them to death" (Wyer, Gaylord, & Grove, 1987, p. 7). As Melton et al. (1997) describe it: "Until well into the 19th century, custody was routinely perceived as a concomitant of the father's power; children, like wives, were in effect the father's chattels" (p. 487).

Since English law tended to shape American law, paternal superiority was continued in the United States throughout the 19th century. In the 1880s, however, judges began to enter orders that, by common law, moved toward making the parental rights secondary to the interests of the children, albeit this happened only when there was significant parental misconduct or the child was being subjected to harm.

By the beginning of the 20th century, public policy shifted and, in custody disputes, the courts began to give preference to mothers:

> The doctrine of maternal preference had a practical basis: Unless a wet nurse could be obtained, a weaned infant might not survive the primitive techniques of artificial feeding available before the 1920s. (Nurcombe & Partlett, 1994, p. 90)

Much like the use of a wet nurse, laws have changed to avoid the gender of the parent being a determinative factor. More will be said about this issue.

Also in the past (up until the 1970s approximately), the courts accepted a presumption that children, particularly those of "tender years" (which meant approximately younger than age seven or so), could best be cared for by their mother. By today's standards, the notion seems antiquated, but in that era the father was presumed to be incapable of providing "that tender care which nature requires, and which it is the peculiar province of a mother to supply" (*Miner v. Miner*, 1849, p. 49).

Even today, the parents themselves often tacitly accept the premise that the children should live with the mother. Warshak (1992) believes that this premise reflects a cultural prescription, based on the assumption that: "(1) Women, by nature, make better parents than men, and (2) Mothers are more important to children than are fathers" (p. 18).

Regarding the issue of maternal superiority, the presumption was conditioned upon "fitness." That is, the father, with the burden of proof, could introduce evidence to suggest that the mother had character deficits, misconduct, and so on, that would justify the court's rejecting both the maternal preference and tender years presumptions. Obviously this amounted to drawing the battle line in the sands of divorce proceedings, a line that some pundits would maintain has never been erased—or even noticeably smudged!

Current statutes, with minor exceptions, make it clear that custody should not be determined by the gender of the parent, even for a child of tender years. Giving males and females equal rights has an interesting origin: "Ironically, the women's movement has resulted in a weakening of the maternal preferences" (Melton et al., 1997, p. 487). On the other hand, judicial discretion, which allows considerable latitude for interpretation of a statute and weighting of the evidence that is presented relevant to the best interests of the child, is still vulnerable to the presumption that the mother has, by her gender, a potential superiority for child care, especially for young children. Indeed, Brinson and Hess (1987) hold that the mother receives custody in the "overwhelming majority" of cases (this may, of course, be due to more than just a gender preference per se). In addition to the presumption that a mother is best able to provide care and nurturing, they allege that there are "prejudices and assumptions of the court and attorneys" (p. 110) influencing the custody outcome, saying:

> Attorneys frequently encourage fathers to negotiate a settlement in which the mother retains custody of the children

and the fathers are given visitation rights, since many attorneys feel that if the case goes before a judge, custody will be awarded to the mother. This assumption of inferior opportunity for custody by fathers may be unfounded in that of the 10 percent contested custody cases that go before the court, fathers retain custody of their children in about half of the cases. While this is a relatively small percentage of the total custody awards, it suggests that a father seeking custody, with the proper preparation, will stand an equal chance of being awarded custody. This is particularly true when it involves children over five or six years old. (p. 110)

The years that have passed since Brinson and Hess issued this opinion have witnessed other events that seemingly equate the opportunity for custody irrespective of parental gender. For example, women continue to enter the work force in greater numbers, thereby allowing fathers an equal opportunity to spend time with their children and establish evidence of child care.

Nonetheless, ill-founded and prejudicial ideas continue in child custody cases. At a recent family law conference, the keynote speaker stated unabashedly: "I do not believe that any father can care for a young girl as well as the mother." Interestingly, soon thereafter the same attorney represented a father in an effort to wrest custody of a young girl away from the mother. The father's attorney entered no allegations of neglect or abuse by the mother, but asserted only that the father could provide the girl with the best custodial parenting (buttressed by the father's having greater wealth than the mother, which presumably would mean the child would receive sociocultural enrichment)—the custody was not, however, changed, but the child support was increased! The attorney was, of course, simply fulfilling his legally defined role, namely to advocate the legal interests of his client, regardless of the personal views that he expressed at the family law conference.

In much the same vein, certain judges continue to give minimal weight to the bulk of the evidence, and give maximum weight to their personal attitudes about parenting, which are often aligned with gender preferences. This statement is not intended to be disrespectful of the court; it is simply a reminder of the human nature that pervades child custody legal proceedings, including what emanates from the bench.

Finally on this matter, Warshak (1992) states: "The motherhood mystique is so entrenched in our culture that most courts will grant custody to a father only if the mother grossly neglects or abuses her children" (p. 20); and "Clearly, our society regards divorced fathers as second-class parents" (p. 20). From personal experience in domestic law, this assertion seems a bit strong, but it does uncover a vulnerability that must be avoided by mental health practitioners.

➡️ *Guideline: If a parent's gender is addressed in child custody testimony, the mental health practitioner should have a scholarly and behavioral science basis for interpretations, opinions, and recommendations that pertain to gender (e.g., derived from research on child development).*

FAMILY RIGHTS

The United States Supreme Court has created a right of privacy (e.g., *Meyer v. Nebraska*, 1923; *Pierce v. Society of Sisters*, 1925). As relevant to child custody, the result has been a hallowed "zone of privacy" for family life, which the court in *Prince v. Massachusetts* (1944) described as "A private realm of family life which the state cannot enter" (p. 166). There are, however, certain reasons and conditions that allow the state (i.e., the government) to penetrate this zone of privacy.

Imposing a law that intrudes on the sanctity of the family could affront individual and parental rights, yet the premium placed on protecting the safety and development of the child calls for legal entrée. Based on the premise that children and youth are human resources and that their protection (development, health, and welfare) is essential to the betterment of society, the safeguarding of children allows for considerable governmental control. That is, public policy holds that the protection of children and youth justifies governmental intrusion into the family's Constitutionally related zone of privacy. Dickson (1995) sets the stage: "Generally parents make most decisions for their children free from interference by the state, in part shielded by a Fourteenth Amendment privacy right" (p. 294). He continues, however, pointing out that family privacy is not unlimited: "The state may impose regulations to protect children from abuse and neglect, intervene to require regulations to life-preserving medical treatment, and remove children from the home for their protection or because their parents are incapable of exercising parental control, among other actions" (p. 248). When a crisis, such as a divorce of the parents, portends to impact negatively on a child, society recognizes that the privacy rights of the parents or family must be made secondary to child protection; therefore, intervention by the legal system is justified.

Because of the hallowed nature of the right of privacy, the decision to intrude legally into the family is considered a major issue. Thus, "State intervention in the private affairs of the family through adjudication of alterations in custodial rights and responsibilities, including possible removal of a child from a parental home, often conflicts with the state's interest in preserving family autonomy" (Wyer et al., 1987, p. 4).

Regardless of the foregoing, child placement laws must be created, implemented, and enforced:

> Child placement laws are designed to ensure for all children an environment that adequately serves their needs. The degree of state intervention on the private ordering of the parent-child relationship ranges from a minimum— automatic assignment of a child by birth certificate to her biological parents—to a maximum—court-ordered removal of a child from her "parents" because she is found to be "abused" or "delinquent," or they are found "unfit" to be parents. The traditional goal of such interventions is to serve "the best interests of the child." In giving meaning to this goal, decision-makers in law must recognize the necessity of protecting a child's psychological as well as physical well-being as guides to placement. Both well-beings are important. Any sharp distinction between them is artificial. (J. Goldstein et al., 1996, p. 5)

Intervention in family life by the government, therefore, is predicated on protecting and supporting the child's development so as to produce human resources for the constructive maintenance and evolution of society.

If and when the government intrudes in the family, there must be a reasonable, perhaps even compelling, justification. Given family rights, any justification should maximize family integrity and minimize governmental power. According to J. Goldstein et al. (1996), there are seven grounds for governmental intervention via child custody proceedings. First, as is common with a dissolution of marriage, the parents can petition the court to determine custody. Second, some parents find that they cannot care adequately for their child (be it due to financial problems or character deficits). These first two options reflect a voluntary willingness for governmental intrusion into family life. Third, an extraneous source (e.g., a social service agency) may attempt to interrupt family relations, and the court will need to take control of the situation. Fourth, a child may be abandoned, whether by death or disappearance of the parents. Fifth, a child may be abused or subjected to conditions that will likely create serious bodily injury, which the parents cannot manage. Sixth, the parent(s) may refuse essential medical care, placing the child at risk of illness or death or depriving the child of treatment that society would deem necessary to assure the healthy development and life. Seventh, circumstances may necessitate that the child have legal representation. The last four options are, of course, intended to safeguard the child's bonding with family or other caregivers, and assure healthy development.

All of foregoing options contradict the autonomy and authority of the parents. Public policy recognizes, however, that the conditions or factors underlying those options for governmental intervention potentially supercede individual or family rights.

➔ *Guideline: The mental health practitioner should honor the legitimacy of a governmental incursion into the family's right of privacy, but should not allow his or her professional services to unnecessarily or inappropriately violate family rights.*

DEVELOPMENTAL CONSIDERATIONS

When it comes to the development of children, psychological theory is anything but unified. There is a plethora of theories. Each theory has its body of "scientific" research, which becomes the subject of debate between advocates and opponents. Regrettably, as with other areas of discordant psychological theories (e.g., behavior therapy versus insight therapy), many times Theory A is justified by denouncing the scholarly status of Theory B.

Although preference is given (as stated in Chapter 2) to the cognitive social-learning and family systems approaches, it would serve little constructive purpose to restrict the substance of this book to only these two theoretical approaches to child development. Rather, consideration will be given to what various theoretical positions contribute to a mental health perspective about children and youth who are subjected to child custody proceedings.

The behavioral viewpoint holds, generally, that the development of a child is a product of genetics and reinforcements. In other words, given biological potentials, the child experiences situations that encourage or discourage certain inclinations, attitudes, and behaviors. Characterizing the child as a passive recipient of the parents' preferences, as manifested in child-rearing practices, does not account for the influences and opportunities that occur when the child is outside the family unit. Such a characterization fails to adequately recognize environmental influences.

As the child ventures forth from the family into the "big wide world," such as entry into a day-care facility, certain genetic potentials are cultivated, while others are neglected. This biologically based construction continues throughout life, albeit that the organism varies at different life stages in its malleability due to environmental factors.

Beyond the genetic or biological potentials, the child engages, by design or happenstance, in social interactions. Being in the presence of others, be it children or adults, provides the child with information that can have a positive, negative, or inconsequential influence on how the child perceives, thinks, and acts. Modern behavior theory does, in fact, accept that the human organism is shaped by social or environmental reinforcers, as consistent with the cognitive social-learning and family systems ideas presented in Chapter 2.

While rooted in psychoanalytic theory, J. Goldstein et al. (1996)* offer a reasonably holistic framework for child development, as potentially applicable to formulating notions about child custody:

1. Unlike adults, children change constantly, from one stage of growth to another. They change with regard to their understanding of events, their tolerance for frustration, and their needs for and demands on parents' care for support, stimulation, guidance, and restraint. These

---

demands vary as the child matures and is capable of independence (that is, gradual freedom from control). Since none of the child's needs remains stable, what serves her developmental interests at one level may be detrimental to her progression at another level.

2. Unlike adults, who measure the passing of time by clock and calendar, children have their own built-in time sense, based on the urgency of their instinctual and emotional needs and on the limits of their cognitive capacities. This results in their intolerance for postponement of gratification and their sensitivity to the length of separations.

3. Unlike adults, young children experience events as happening solely with reference to their own persons. Thus they may experience the birth of a sibling as an act of parental hostility; the emotional preoccupation or illness of a parent as rejection; or the death or involuntary absence of a parent as intentional abandonment.

4. Unlike adults, children are governed in much of their functioning by the irrational parts of their minds—their primitive wishes and impulses. Consequently, they respond to any threat to their emotional security with reactions that do not help them to cope, but rather put them at the mercy of events.

5. Unlike adults, children have no psychological conception of blood-tie relationships until quite late in their development. For the biological parents, the experience of conceiving, carrying, and giving birth prepares them to feel close to and responsible for their child. These considerations carry no weight with children, who are emotionally unaware of the events leading to their existence. What matters to them is the pattern of day-to-day interchanges with the adults who take care of them and who, on the strength of such interactions, become the parent figures to whom they are attached. (p. 9)

This position accepts that children differ considerably, and that a particular child may or may not fit clearly into the preceding developmental framework.

➡ *Guideline: In formulating interpretations, opinions, and recommendations for child custody proceedings, the mental health
practitioner should clearly identify and astutely evaluate the
child's idiosyncratic developmental qualities, needs, and potentials.*

While the family is fundamental to social development, the child
is shaped by environmental influences, perhaps with even greater
power than emanates from family life. As stated earlier, environmental influences vary from stage to stage, and some behavioral
scientists (including myself) believe that social development is
particularly influential when the child reaches adolescence.

From the family systems perspective, a dysfunctional child
represents problems within the family. The pathology of the family
system may be manifested by the child; that is, the child's symptoms represent problematic issues within the family (Zilbach, 1986).
Certainly children exposed to divorced parents and reconstituted
family situations face an elevated risk of being the repository for
reinforced dysfunctional behavior. For example, the child may,
through lineal notions of causality among the estranged parents,
become the family scapegoat (Worden, 1999).

Later, guidelines will be offered for mental health interventions that will rely on and meld strategies from the cognitive social-
learning and family systems approach. For now, it is sufficient to
restate what was set forth in Chapter 2, namely that any sort of
conceptualization, assessment, opinion, or intervention connected
to testimony or other mental health services in a child custody case
should rely on principles from cognitive social-learning and family
systems.

Chapter 4

ENTERING THE LEGAL ARENA

Custody-related decisions are based on legislative and common (or case) law. The prevailing public policy supports that the parents should be part of the decision-making process, but only if it is in the best interests of the child. Also, the commitment to possible involvement of both parents in the lives of their children is reflected in the growing public policy encouragement of mediation services for divorcing parents. In some states, mediation may now be legally mandated, or at least expected unless contradicted by the facts of the particular case.

Despite the public policy support for involving the parents in the decision making about custody, parents are not given unfettered decision making about the circumstances for the postdivorce lives of their children. Any decision made by the parents, such as with whom the child will have primary residential custody, must pass inspection by the court. Usually this means that evidence supporting the parental decision must be presented to the court, and be adjudged as being both conscionable and in the best interests of the child. In other words, any agreement between the parents must be wise, logical, and dedicated to the well-being of the child.

The fact that parents do not have total decision-making authority over their children often fuels the dispute between the parents. That is, being chagrined about the pending change in the parent-child relationship occasioned by the divorce, a parent resents having the court pass judgment on what he or she believes should be solely a parental determination. In these instances, sublimation and displacement seem to occur, namely loss of parental authority leads one or both parents to become more contemptuous toward the other parent and motivated to battle over child custody issues. Faced with unwanted court scrutiny, a parent often launches an ill-conceived effort to one-up the other parent, and the litigation is intensified.

Despite what child custody legal proceedings may foster within and between the parents, the emotional backdrop of divorce will increase the court's control, rather than acceptance of parental preferences. This problem is, seemingly, appropriate for the mental health practitioner to consider and deal with when providing professional services. Hopefully the mental health practitioner will realize, and help the parents to realize, that court scrutiny is a necessity, not an assault on parental rights.

To help both parents (and other family members as well) cooperate with and accept the child custody legal proceedings, thereby cooling the emotions and lessening the war by litigation, the mental health practitioner should emphasize the parental role in supplying the information that will be used for the child custody testimony. Relying on the parents accomplishes four important purposes. First, meaningful participation by both parents will help them "own" (i.e., accept) the mental health practitioner's testimony and the ultimatum by the court. Second, it will lessen the possibility of hostile or closed communications toward child custody issues and the mental health practitioner, and will enhance the quality of information made available to the mental health practitioner for purposes of testimony. Third, it will presumably foster more positive postdivorce relations between the parents, thereby contributing their meeting the best interests of the child. Fourth, if the parents sense that their views have been heard and valued, and that their rights have been honored, the possibility of an ethical, regulatory, or legal complaint against the mental health practitioner will be less likely.

➔ *Guideline: The mental health practitioner should assertively encourage, pursue, and respect meaningful involvement by the parents in the collection of information for assessment and the formulation of interpretations, opinions, and recommendations that will be used in the child custody testimony.*

No authoritative public policy or legal source disputes that parents should be allowed an opportunity to try to self determine the custody-related conditions for the postdivorce lives of their children. If the parents cannot agree on custody conditions, the custody matter must be put to the court. Again, the court considers evidence that is in accord with the rules of evidence and civil procedure, state statutes, and appellate court rulings (all of which must be applicable to the particular jurisdiction).

JUDICIAL DISCRETION

Notwithstanding the foregoing legal cornerstones, the trial judge always has considerable discretion. That is, an appellate court recognizes that the trial judge had the benefit of firsthand interaction with the parties and the children, which creates an important basis for the legal judgments. Therefore, unless there is reversible error (e.g., based on a procedural error, or abuse of discretion), an appellate ruling commonly shows deference to the trial court.

Through an order (a point-in-time judgment about certain issues) or a decree (a final adjudication of all issues), the judge makes determinations pertaining to child custody, visitation, child support, and other matters. The decision-making process is, however, strongly influenced—but not totally dictated—by legislation. For example, in addition to a statutory definition and appellate rulings on criteria for the best interests of the child, the trial court may have certain guidelines for issues, such as how to compute child support according to the respective incomes of the parents or what is the "standard" visitation schedule.

Among the states, the legislation pertaining to child custody is currently highly similar. However, each jurisdiction can and usually does have uniqueness(es). The uniqueness for a state-level jurisdiction can come from the wording of the legislation or the lineage of appellate cases that define the statute(s).

As might be inferred from the earlier comments about judicial discretion, to some extent the uniqueness comes from the particular judge assigned to hear a given custody case: "The judge has broad discretion to weigh any factor that may be relevant in determining which parent's custody will promote the child's welfare" (Scott & Emery, 1987, p. 27). Botein (1952) elaborates:

The role of the trial court is to determine the best interests of the child based on the adversarial presentation of evidence. The lives and personalities of at least two adults and one child are telescoped and presented to him in a few hours. From this capsule presentation he must decide where lie the best interests of the child or, very often, which parent will harm the child the least. The judge's verdict is distilled from the hardest kind of fact finding. From sharply disputed evidence, he must predict the future conduct of parents on his appraisal of their past conduct. (p. 424)

As will emerge, the contemporary trial court typically relies heavily upon mental health practitioners (and other experts) for the evidence upon which judicial orders and decrees will be based. As a bottom line to the issue of judicial discretion, when receiving evidence, such as expert testimony from a mental health professional, two judges in the same courthouse could differ in the weight given to certain evidentiary points.

➔ *Guideline: In child custody proceedings, the mental health practitioner must accept that the judge has discretion to weigh testimony; is the designated source for answering the ultimate legal question (e.g., which parent should have residential custody, what should be the visitation schedule); and can issue orders and decrees that must be honored fully by the mental health practitioner.*

FEDERAL LEGISLATION

As will be discussed throughout this book, the so-called "best interests of the child" test dominates child custody legal proceedings. It is rooted in the Uniform Marriage and Divorce Act (UMDA), approved by the American Bar Association in 1974: "Adopted wholly or in modified form by most states, the UMDA contains a section concerning the best interests criteria which represent a distillation of contemporary thinking on the matter" (Nurcombe & Partlett, 1994, p. 91).

Considerable importance must be attributed to "Uniform Acts," such as (but not limited to) the Uniform Child Custody Jurisdiction Act (UCCJA, 1979), Uniform Marriage and Divorce Act (UMDA, 1974), Uniform Parentage Act (UPA, 1979), and Uniform Putative and Unknown Father Act (UPUFA, 1988). Of course there are many other laws both at the state and federal levels that have authority, in one way or another, over what occurs in child custody cases, such as (but again not limited to) the federal Parental Kidnapping Prevention Act (PKPA, 1980), and Family Support Act (FSA, 1988). Although there is a myriad of federal laws that potentially connect to child custody matters, the state legislative and judicial systems still have the foremost role in legal determinations.

For some years now, it appears that the Uniform Child Custody Jurisdiction Act (UCCJA) has strongly influenced, perhaps even dominated, state statutory law. Brinson and Hess (1987) describe the UCCJA as follows:

> The UCCJA provides a uniform framework around which custodial issues may be developed, thereby encouraging consistency in rulings across jurisdictions. In establishing a criteria [sic] for determination of custody, the UCCJA suggests the application of the following: (1) the age and sex of the child; (2) the wishes of the child as to his custodian; (3) interactions and interrelationships of the child with parents, siblings, and significant others; (4) the child's adjustment to home, school, and community; and (5) the mental and physical health of all parties involved. The clinician can provide valuable input to the court on a number of these issues. (p. 109)

Throughout this book, there is discussion about the best interests of the child; and in the next chapter, more specifics will be given about the factors or criteria that constitute the best interests of the child test, as would be potentially the substance of testimony by a mental health practitioner. At this point, recall that modern thinking about family systems supports that the best interests of the child must be placed against a backdrop of the familial interactions and influences.

➔ *Guideline: The mental health practitioner should be knowledgeable about federal and state statutory and case law that pertain to child custody issues, especially (but not limited to) the criteria considered by the particular jurisdiction to constitute the best interests of the child test.*

JUDICIAL DETERMINATIONS

Although federal acts and state statutes cast a mold for judicial decisions, the discretion allowed to the judge means that the message may be legislative guidance. Interpretations must be made by the judge, the trier of fact (note that a jury is also a trier of fact, but use of jury for a custody matter rarely occurs).

While society anoints the judge with an "all knowing" status for decision making, in point of fact the human nature of the judge enters into the processing of the information and the judgments. Rohman, Sales, and Lou (1987) point out that it is "not surprising that judges have had great difficulty implementing the best interests standards without bringing in their own values for child rearing and family life" (p. 92).

Making custody-related decisions is a tremendous burden placed on and accepted by the judge. From the evidence admitted, the judge has to adduce conditions that will occur in the future. More than one judge has said the obvious, to wit: "I need a crystal ball to determine which parent can best meet the child's interests." Such speculation, prognostication, and determination flies in the face of what is preferred by behavioral scientists. Although stated throughout this book, it is important to underscore that society has not ordained mental health practitioners to express nonscholarly or nonscientific views—society has designated only the judge for subjective and personalized decisions.

→ *Guideline: The mental health practitioner must accept that society (through its laws) has designated only the judge to render subjective and personalized decisions.*

The judge stoically performs the delicate yet weighty tasks. An apt description of the judicial burden is given by J. Goldstein et al. (1996):

> The speculative nature of the task clearly cannot absolve judges from responsibility for exercising their judgment about what, according to the evidence, augurs best at that point for the balance of the childhood. It can, however, and should, in deciding the incidents of custody, give pause about the extent to which judges interpose themselves between the child and the parent responsible for exercising, on a daily basis, the kind of judgment a judge is called upon to make

only once. The parent, not the judge, will be left to live with the daily consequences of caring for the child within the limits of that once judicial pronouncement." (p. 36)

The latter point commonly underlies the well-known judicial statement that: "The best custody determination will displease both parents." That is, the parent senses that, regardless of what custody or visitation arrangement has been ordered by the judge, the parent-child relationship will be permanently altered by this external source (i.e., the judge), as opposed to being self determined by the parent. Here again (similar to a parent's resenting a loss of self determination to court scrutiny), negative feelings about the permanent alteration of the parent-child relationship may subliminally motivate one or both parents towards contentiousness and litigiousness.

If the statute does not set forth criteria that disqualifies one of the parents, both parents are presumably suitable or (to use the old-fashioned term) "fit" to have custody of the child: "Thus, in resolving custodial disputes between such fit parents, a judge must necessarily call upon his or her culturally determined notions about what type of upbringing might be best for a child" (Wyer et al., 1987, p. 4). This paves the way, of course, for the judge to seek information, such as from behavioral science concepts expressed by professionals, to wit: expert opinions from mental health practitioners.

→ *Guideline: In the event that the judge seeks information from the mental health practitioner that is of a nature that would not be consonant with professional ethics and standards, the mental health practitioner should respectfully state reservations and make a pronounced effort to limit or qualify the testimony.*

From social theory, it is clear that judicial decision making is a powerful influence on the evolution of our society. Being an amorphous collection of values, beliefs, attitudes, and ethics, public policy shapes the law-making process, such as how statutory law is fashioned by legislators. In turn, the judicial system acts upon statutory law, creating judge-made or common law in day-to-day case determinations. The decision by a judge in a child custody case loops back to public policy, and the social cycle continues—or as Fanshel (1957) described it: "The handling of the matter of the disposition of a human life can both reflect that society as well as act back upon it" (p. 80).

THE ADVERSARIAL APPROACH

From the mental health perspective, there is reason to question whether the adversarial nature of child custody disputes contributes positively to the furtherance of healthy family relations subsequent to the divorce: "While the objective of the law is to resolve the custody issue in a manner that will be in the child's best interests, the legal process may have a destructive impact on both child and parents" (Scott & Emery, 1987, p. 23). The profound acrimony that is inherent to child custody disputes leads many mental health practitioners, attorneys, and judges to prefer to avoid involvement in custody disputes.

Before becoming an attorney, I had worked considerably as a psychologist in custody cases. After graduating from law school and being admitted to the bar to practice law, I continued to expect that I would work in custody-related cases. In my first few years as an attorney, numerous attorneys and judges commented to me that, despite my commitment to the family law area, "I'll bet it won't be long before you want to do something other than divorce and custody cases." At the time I doubted their predictions, but now I know that my legal colleagues were right.

Despite my psychology training and experience, as well as my personal dedication to enhancing family life in our society, I experienced considerable "wear and tear" on my professional motivations, and soon lessened my work with child custody cases. Among legalists, working with divorce and custody is not an attractive option. Regrettably but not surprisingly, the current elevated risk of ethics, regulatory, and legal complaints from parents involved in custody litigation has led increasing numbers of mental health practitioners to decrease, resist, or reject providing custody-related services. Nonetheless, professional ethics and standards support that mental health practitioners should contribute to child custody cases; and legal process (e.g., subpoenas and court orders) make it virtually impossible for a mental health practitioner to refuse involvement in child custody legal proceedings.

➔ *Guideline: Despite the negatives and risks associated with child custody cases, there is reason for the mental health practitioner to fulfill the social responsibility to be of service, and the mental health practitioner should accept that legal process (e.g.,*

*subpoenas and court orders) makes it unlikely that child cus-
tody cases can or should be avoided in total.*

The factor that makes a child custody dispute so unpleasant is
the irrational and destructive emotionality that is encountered. Using a euphemism, "During a divorce and custody dispute, both
parents are crazy." Needless to say, such emotionality leads to psychological defense mechanisms, such as sublimation, projection,
and displacement, that contribute considerably to the propensity for
filing ethics, regulatory, and legal complaints against the mental
health practitioners who offer testimony, voluntarily or by legal
process, as therapists, evaluators, mediators, and experts.

➜ *Guideline: When working in a child custody case, the mental
health practitioner should recognize, consider, and weigh the
probable effects of the adversarial context; that is, the mental
health practitioner should acknowledge that the information
relevant to, say, a parent's emotions, personality, and conduct
may not be a reflection of that parent's qualities in a non-
adversarial context.*

The reason that unhealthy and harmful emotionality is en-
demic to divorce and custody cases is simple:

In most litigation the adversaries are strangers, business
associates, or acquaintances. The divorcing couple's prior
intimate relationship exaggerates from the outset the potential for hostility. Because of the prior relationship, each
parent may know particularly hurtful and damaging facts
about the other. (Scott & Emery, 1987, p. 27)

As a result of the emotionality, it is commonplace for persons who
have been prototypes of civility, intelligence, good judgment, and
constructive conduct to lose all semblance of those blessings when
they are subjected to a divorce and, even more so, a custody dispute. Again, it is easy to see how the emotionality breeds ethics,
regulatory, and legal complaints.

Coping effectively with life in good times is difficult enough.
Persons facing a divorce also see their emotional and financial resources depleted rapidly and dramatically, which results in uncommon ineffectiveness. Not only will the divorce modify or destroy a
once-coveted personal identity (that of being both spouse and par-

ent), the threat of losing control of the nature and amount of contact with one's children cuts to the fiber of self worth. Predictably, the all-too-common result is desperate, illogical, unhealthy, and destructive emotionality. Regrettably, this extraordinary emotionality creates detrimental effects to self and the children.

➔ *Guideline: Regardless of the role definition for involvement in the child custody case, the mental health practitioner should strive to ward off detrimental effects from the extraordinary emotions; that is, an acceptable goal is to ameliorate emotionality to benefit all persons who are part of the child's present and future family system.*

More and more disputes between the parties over custody-related issues are occurring. Wyer et al. (1987) pinpoint what may well be one of the causes of the modern epidemic of child custody disputes:

> The vagueness of the best interests of the child standard affords broad discretion to trial courts and limits appellate review. The heavily factual nature of the standard requires case-by-case determination and allows little purely legal precedent to develop. Thus prospective litigants cannot easily predict what courts will decide. This lack of predictability has been criticized as the cause for an increase in custody litigation. (p. 14)

They muse, however, that: "While it may be a reasonable criticism, there is no guarantee that greater predictability would discourage litigation, particularly in such an emotionally charged area" (p. 14).

TYPES OF CHILD CUSTODY ARRANGEMENTS

Although child custody legal disputes are substantial in number, the most common arrangement for child custody is still for the parents to agree about with whom the child will live (i.e., physical or residential custody), which means that there is no need to present a dispute to the court. It would seem that this arrangement might carry less adverse emotionality than putting a dispute to the court to decide. Given human nature, this is not necessarily true. It may be that circumstances basically force one of the parents to accept or reject the custody arrangement. That is, the parents could agree on the custody placement for other than the best interests of the child. Because of this risk to children, child custody arrangements should always be subject to scrutiny by the court.

➜ *Guideline: The mental health practitioner should not (e.g., when serving as a mediator) sanction a child custody agreement reached by parents that is not clearly in the best interests of the child, and should encourage submitting less-than-desirable agreements for judicial review and approval.*

PARENTAL AGREEMENTS

As mentioned earlier, any child custody arrangement upon which the parents agree is always subject to the review and approval of the court. That is, if the parents were to agree on a custody and/or visitation plan that the court thought was not in the best interests of the child—such as the idea that the child would live 3½ days with one parent and then move to the other parent's home for 3½ days—the court could (and likely would) refuse to accept the parental plan.

If the parental preferences or agreement were not accepted, the court might suggest that the parents reconsider the options that are available. This suggestion might well be accompanied by some rather direct guidance from the judge as to what the court believes to be in the best interests of the child. It is not unusual for the judge to summon the attorneys into his or her chambers, without the parties being present, and give specific directions about what should be in a child custody agreement and how the attorneys should convince their respective clients accordingly.

Although the foregoing exercise of authority by the judge may seem a bit heavy-handed and a possible affront to the parents' right to present evidence in the courtroom, judicial guidance is not necessarily a bad thing. Being apprised of the family situation, the judge is revealing to the attorneys what sort of order or decree would likely be entered. Although the attorneys know that the outcome is almost certain, they can convey the judicial views in a way that will allow the parents to sense they are making the final decision about the litigation, which will cultivate a personal acceptance of the outcome for each parent. Of course, if the parents seem to be deadlocked (or impervious to the best interests of the child), the court might refer the parents to a mediator or get exasperated and, without further ado, order what the judge decides is in the best interests of the children. Simply put, if the judge offers guidance to the attorneys, the parents would do well to heed the message.

Although the large majority of child custody arrangements are decided by the parents, it is predictable that changes will have to be considered in later months or years. For example, as the child gets older, such as becoming a teenager, the situation tilts away from parental preferences to the child's preferences. More will be said about this matter in a later chapter.

ALTERNATING, DIVIDED, AND SPLIT CUSTODY

Some parents want some sort of alternating or divided custody arrangement (this should not be confused with joint custody, which will be discussed subsequently). In general, courts seem to frown on the idea of a child's residing in more than one place, even if it is with both natural parents (Warshak, 1992). Brinson and Hess (1987) point out: "Critics of divided custody generally believe that it creates confusion for the child with regard to authority and that shifting the child from home to home results in an unstable environment with lack of permanent associations for the child" (p. 111). Warshak (1992) cautions: "It is easy for parents to fool themselves into thinking that a split-custody arrangement is best for the children when it may really be a poor compromise between unyielding parents" (p. 200).

Perhaps the foremost criterion for child custody determinations is continuity or stability of living for the child, which is contrary to alternating or divided custody. By its very nature, a divided custody arrangement that would involve the child's moving back and forth between homes every few days contradicts the ideas of continuity or stability of living, and is rarely approved by the court.

At the same time, the mental health perspective supports that both parents should have frequent and meaningful involvement with the child (assuming that each parent will, in fact, offer positive conditions to the child). There are, however, numerous research studies that "have found little relationship between frequency of child/nonresidential parent contact and child's postdivorce adjustment" (Bogolub, 1995, p. 17). Therefore, the aforementioned mental health perspective that both parents should have frequent and meaningful involvement with the child may or may not be justified. The family systems approach, however, supports the child's having frequent and meaningful involvement with both parents.

→ *Guideline: In accord with the child's receiving lifelong developmental benefits from his or her family system, the mental health practitioner should endorse, unless it reasonably contradicts the best interests of the child, that both parents will continue to have frequent and meaningful involvement with the child.*

Ideally, the parents would agree that the child would travel between the two residences in a reasonable and constructive manner (assuming each parent can provide appropriate living accommodations and allot time to be with the child). A judicial order or decree that designates the child's primary residential custody to be with one parent does not usually preclude the parents' implementing an informal residential arrangement, as long as the noncustodial parent has not been adjudged to pose a risk to the child and the moves are in the best interests of the child. It must be emphasized, however, that any self-made arrangements by parents must not contradict an order issued by the court.

→ *Guideline: When dealing with a postdivorce family, the mental health practitioner should not endorse any arrangement affecting the child that contradicts an order issued by the court.*

There are some instances when a court approves a so-called split custody arrangement; that is, the court endorses and orders the parents' having divided residential custody. This rarity usually occurs only when the evidence strongly supports that shifting the child back and forth between the parents' two homes will be best for the child.

If there is more than one child, there are (also rare) occasions when the court will give primary custody of one child (or certain children) to one parent and primary custody of another child (or other children) to the other parent, and possibly even allow the children to shift back and forth between the two residences. Judges only cautiously allow these unusual situations, and only when the parents have provided convincing evidence that they are individually and together psychologically up to the arrangements, and that the children will benefit.

So-called split custody involves placing some of the children with one parent and some of the children with the other parent. Separating siblings introduces developmental concerns. Because of the myriad of possible considerations, there is no definitive research to simplify the task for child custody testimony. Warshak (1992) illustrates the problem:

> Generally, the greater the age difference between siblings, the more likely a split-custody arrangement might be to serve their needs. But many other factors need to be taken into account. Some siblings who are far apart in ages are very closely bonded. Other siblings, who are very close in age, have such an intense rivalry that they make each other miserable. In some families, each parent has a much better relationship with one child than with another. (p. 199)

Overwhelmingly, judges seem to believe that siblings should be kept together. When the parents and/or children advocate otherwise, judges tend to be anything but sanguine. With split custody on the horizon, the court would be apt to seek specific information, such as from a mental health professional, as to the advisability of dividing the siblings among the parents.

Common sense alone supports that siblings benefit from being together, and development theory (as well as the consistency/stability criterion) buttresses this viewpoint. Separating siblings is most often justified by pragmatics, rather than by psychological theory.

There are certain practical circumstances that make split custody appropriate. Even then, the separation of the children is more often based on negatives than an expectation that the children will best thrive by being apart. In other words, practical considerations might make a split-custody arrangement the least-detrimental alternative. It could be that: the children have different degrees of bonding (for whatever healthy or unhealthy reason) with the two parents; special needs for one child (say, a child's attending a particular school or having medical services available) would support his or her being with one parent, while the other children live with the other parent; or financial conditions may necessitate the children be separated—the list could go on.

In one case, a 16-year-old had dropped out of school and been arrested several times, and the custodial parent was bewildered. Although the court had, at the time of divorce, placed all of the children with one parent, the delinquency record led the court to modify the custody of the one problem youth, changing the custody to the other parent to avoid negative influences for the other children in the family and to maximize the possibility of effective parenting.

➡ *Guideline: When the mental health practitioner is asked to opine about any unusual custody arrangement, the fundamental posture of requiring scholarly and behavior science information for a professional opinion becomes critically important; therefore, unless there are persuasive geographical or other negative conditions (e.g., continuing animosity and legal warfare between the parents) that preclude the child's having frequent and positive contact between all of the siblings and both parents, the mental health practitioner should oppose dividing the siblings into separate homes.*

JOINT CUSTODY

When parents divorce and reality sets in that it is probable that only one parent will have primary residential custody of the child, the parent who is likely to not receive the primary residential custody thinks immediately about joint custody:

> Technically, *joint custody* refers to shared parental authority to make decisions on behalf of children. It does not necessarily include joint physical custody; indeed, such an arrangement is far less common than joint legal custody. (Melton et al., 1997, p. 490)

Granted, many of the early proponents of joint custody, such as advocacy groups for fathers and the legislators who were enlisted to create enabling laws, believed that both legal authority over and shared physical custody of the child would occur—but this viewpoint was never embraced fully by the judicial system. Recall, however, the negative statements made earlier about alternative, split, divided custody.

The positive premise for joint custody is that, notwithstanding the divorce, the parents should continue to have involvement with their children and share in the decision making, minimizing the adverse effects of the divorce and maximizing healthy development for the children: "Specifically, from this viewpoint, joint custody is thought to enhance the well-being of children by fostering their continued relationship with both parents and by eliminating the legal custody battles and adversarial climate that surround sole-custody contests, thereby minimizing their exposure to parental conflict" (Feiner & Terre, 1987, p. 127). This option presumes that the parents can cooperatively fulfill constructive goals.

Although the idea of the parents' continuing to share custody of their children subsequent to a divorce has popular appeal, the barriers between idealism and pragmatism must not be ignored. Specifically, the adverse emotionality that is common to divorce situations, as mentioned several times already, almost preordains failure for joint custody arrangements.

When joint custody first appeared on the family law scene, state legislatures adopted statutes, believing that joint custody would benefit the children of divorce and cut down on the number of postdivorce conflicts and the concomitant legal petitions for modifications of previous judicial orders (which could result in less financial expenditures for the judicial system). Today the majority of states include support for joint custody in statutory law, and, "the more recent statutes tend to have stronger presumptions in favor of joint custody" (Melton et al., 1997, p. 490).

Not uncommon in politically motivated issues, the rising legislative support for joint custody seems somewhat unjustified. Over the years, proof of benefits to any person or the state remains lacking, and judges and parents alike now seem less than enthusiastic about joint custody.

Why is joint custody not more successful? Clearly the answer comes from the fact that the parents moved from a marital union to an adversarial relationship, and the implicit and explicit negativism towards each other is a harbinger of doom for cooperation, even if it is to benefit their children:

> Joint physical custody clearly requires diligent efforts by parents to make it work. It typically results from a significant commitment by both parents to the maintenance of strong parental relationships. Although this dual commitment sometimes reflects a shared belief system about the importance of both parents' involvement, it more commonly reflects the father's insistence on a higher level of involvement than the mother had wished. (Melton et al., 1997, p. 495)

In other words, the idealistic or political motives that were used to formulate joint custody laws do not accurately reflect or accommodate the typical level of parental cooperation.

Effective joint custody places strong demands on the parents. For the child's best interests to be met by joint custody, it is essential that "both parents are able to work out the flexibility, maintain similar environments, and have financial means and geographical proximity to carry out such a plan" (Brinson & Hess, 1987, p. 111).

It is regrettable that, more often than not, the divorce process lessens each parent's capacity to work with the other parent, even when the health and welfare of the children are at stake. In addition to the negative affect (e.g., spite, blame, need for retribution) and counterproductive conduct (e.g., hostile comments, denigration of the other parent, manipulation of visitation), there are pragmatic concerns. As each parent's life goes on, there will be: new significant others or spouses which will impact on the familial dynamics (including the possibility of new children by a subsequent partner); financial and employment ups and downs (including the possibility of the one parent's need to move to another locale); and the likelihood that the child will eventually form his or her own preferences about place of residence.

From the perspective of the law, joint custody in general can potentially honor the rights of each parent, which will presumably maximize each parent's contribution to the best interests of the child. Certain judges seem to favor joint custody because it allows avoiding use of "Solomon's sword," that is, dividing the custody at the risk of injuring the child.

From the perspective of mental health, joint custody arrangements deserve consideration. Also, many, if not all, mental health practitioners who conduct custody evaluations will be asked to address the possibility of joint custody. When this occurs, the mental health practitioner must be cautious to avoid being susceptible to the infectious idealistic appeal. To the contrary, the mental health practitioner should acknowledge the absence of empirical support for joint custody in general. Further, the mental health practitioner must keep in mind the dearth of objective measures of a parent's ability to enter into joint custody. On the latter, any practitioner who is willing to state an opinion about parental ability to engage constructively in a joint custody arrangement will be hard pressed to provide a rationale based on research.

→ *Guideline:* When the mental health practitioner opines about any child custody (or visitation) arrangement, the necessity of scholarly and behavioral science basis for professional opinions must be maintained, which means that it is unlikely, at this point of time, that the mental health practitioner can formulate an adequate scholarly or behavioral science rationale for an opinion about one custody (or visitation) arrangement versus another. Stated differently, public policies and the laws have designated only the judge to be the trier of fact for answering the ultimate legal questions, and the mental health practitioner should restrict testimony (that satisfies professional standards) to information, interpretations, opinions, and recommendations relevant to the ultimate legal questions, and leave the specific answers or determinations to the judge.

Chapter 5

DETERMINING CHILD CUSTODY

Child custody determinations are influenced by public policy, laws, professional ethics and standards, and the personal characteristics of all people who are parties to, affected by, or involved with the legal proceedings. The processes and outcomes are subject to the one-of-a-kind interface between the legal system and mental health services.

THE ROLE OF ATTORNEYS

In child custody cases, the roles for attorneys and mental health professionals are considerably different and discrepant. Rather than assuredly being devoted to healthy family relations, the attorneys are dedicated to maximizing legal rights and benefits for their respective clients. As Scott and Emery (1987) explain: "In representing a parent, the attorney's first obligation is not to protect the child's best interests but to pursue the parent's objectives" (p. 23). In other words, attorneys who are "employed by the parents may focus their energies single-mindedly on winning custody for their clients, regardless of whether such efforts promote the child's welfare" (pp. 23-24).

The foregoing does not mean, however, that all attorneys disregard the best interests of the child. On the contrary, the role of the attorneys involves advising the parents, and as officers of the court, informing the parents that public policy and the law support that the best interest of the child should be paramount.

Dissolution of marriage cases sometimes require the attorney to advocate issues that may not support the best interests of the child. That is, the attorneys are committed to advocacy of other than the best interests of the child, such as how to maximize their respective client's interests relevant to a division of property, alimony, and so on. Sometimes these competing advocacies collide.

An attorney may, therefore, appropriately pursue goals that are inappropriate for a mental health practitioner to either be involved with or support. In fact, certain legal goals that are assigned to the attorney's role could contradict mental health issues, and should be opposed by a mental health practitioner.

Among other strategies, "Attorneys representing husband and wife may advise their clients not to communicate with each other" (Scott & Emery, 1987, p. 24). This advice, to the mental health practitioner, may seem exactly opposite of what would be helpful to strengthening family relations during the divorce crisis. Of course, the attorneys are restricting communications to prevent the occurrence of disadvantageous information or conduct, as would impact negatively on the strategic bargaining. Although the effect on family relations may be negative, the attorneys are not intentionally promoting dysfunction or deleterious conditions for the child.

As detestable as it sounds, some attorneys may encourage the parents to enter into a sham quest for custody: "One parent may threaten litigation of the custody issue to achieve a favorable outcome in the support and property settlement, whether or not custody is actually desired" (Scott & Emery, 1987, p. 24). The mental health practitioner should reject any role or function that does not serve an honest purpose.

➜ *Guideline: The mental health practitioner should be wary of legal efforts that, although perhaps appropriate for the role of an attorney, would be inappropriate for the mental health practitioner to accommodate or support.*

Committed to their respective client's legal interests, the attorneys define their roles according to two opposing approaches, referred to as the best interest model and the advocacy model:

> Under a best interest approach, an attorney acts in a way that maximizes achieving the client's interest even if such

action involves disregard of the client's choice. Under an advocacy approach, the attorney will defer to the client's wishes. (Hermann, 1997, p. 130)

To promote mental health for all concerned, the attorneys in a child custody proceeding should not pause to conclude that the client's interests should prevail, and a client's unhealthy wish should be countered. That is, the interests of the client would surely support positive postdivorce family relations. Thus, even if the clients want warfare with each other, the attorneys would attempt to circumvent it.

For attorneys, ignoring the clients' preferences is not a simple matter. Given the laws and bar ethics that establish the duties for and govern the conduct of attorneys, there may or may not be (depending on the jurisdiction) a formal legal directive toward either model; and in exercising discretion, attorneys incur the distinct risk of complaint to and censure by the bar. When this happens, much like complaints against mental health practitioners, there can be devastating effects imposed on legal careers.

Certainly each attorney must show proper allegiance and advocacy, however defined, to the person retaining his or her services. Therefore, balancing competing interests (e.g., the interests of the parent versus the interests of the child) is often problematic for an attorney.

➔ *Guideline: Depending on the circumstances, the mental health practitioner should be prepared to avoid and perhaps oppose legal strategies that may jeopardize healthy postdivorce family relations.*

THE ROLE OF GUARDIANS

By common law (and typically by statutory law as well), the parents hold the legal rights of the child. Therefore, it is reasonable for all concerned to presume that the parents will safeguard the child's interests. Of course all parents do not adequately safeguard the child's interests. When there is a lapse in child protection, the law opens the door to bringing in a guardian for the child.

When one or both of the parents or attorneys, or the court itself, senses that the legal rights of the parents may be discrepant with the legal rights of the child, the court can appoint a guardian for the child's personal interests and property: "The legal basis for guardianship laws, which mandate the state to care for a person who is unable to care for himself or herself, is the state's *parens patriae* power" (Hermann, 1997, p. 214). This is an example of how society implements protection of its human resources.

Statutes and judicial orders will define the nature and extent of the guardian's authority and role. Even a guardian with plenary (or full) authority will "rarely have unrestricted authority" (Hermann, 1997, p. 223). For example, the guardian appointed to represent a child in a custody dispute might not have temporary residential custody, or might not be able to waive rights on behalf of the child to, say, property.

For the mental health practitioner who is named a guardian, it is important to recognize that the role and functions are not risk free. The guardian can usually be held personally liable for failing to properly represent the interests of the child, albeit that some jurisdictions extend a certain degree of immunity to guardians.

Being a guardian does not, of course, exempt the mental health practitioner from the professional ethics and standards applied to his or her discipline. In some situations, the mental health practitioner may have to request a judicial resolution of a possible conflict between the law and professional ethics and standards. A judicial order that details the role and functions for the guardian is always advisable, and I believe necessary to benefit all concerned.

➔ **Guideline:** *If designated a guardian of a child, the mental health practitioner should: recognize that being a guardian is not assuredly free from legal risk; adhere to professional ethics and standards; and request a judicial order that details the role and functions.*

In child custody legal proceedings, the guardian is usually referred to as the guardian *ad litem* (the acronym, GAL, is often used in documents), which means guardian of the papers. By definition, the guardian is the child's advocate; but the guardian often assumes a quasi-parental attitude (Melton & Lind, 1982).

There is considerable dispute about the proper role for guardians in child custody cases, but certainly remaining objective is essential. That is, the guardian must be free from undue influence from the competing parents. As Scott and Emery (1987) describe it: "At a minimum, the guardian *ad litem* serves to reduce the distortion that may result from the introduction of evidence by the two parents" (p. 32). The guardian should be a prototype for propriety.

→ *Guideline: When serving as a guardian, the mental health practitioner must strive to be objective; in the event that there is undue influence or duress created by either or both of the parents or there is semblance of conflict of interests or other impropriety on the part of the mental health practitioner, the court should be requested to consider allowing the guardian to withdraw from the case.*

INAPPROPRIATE MULTIPLE ROLES

As discussed earlier, an attorney cannot unquestionably provide equal advocacy of the legal interests of one parent and of a child. That is, the attorney cannot serve two purposes, namely attempting to represent clients who might have conflicting interests. Thus, the child may have a guardian appointed by the court.

In the same light, the mental health practitioner who attempts to serve two purposes cannot unquestionably provide fair and objective professional services. The issue of multiple roles will be discussed in greater depth later in this book, but for now introductory consideration should be given to situations in which the court or the parents request the mental health practitioner to serve multiple roles.

Some judges press the mental health practitioner who conducts a court-ordered evaluation to also serve as guardian and/or assume the role of mediator. Such a proposal from a judge can be a heady experience for the mental health practitioner. After all, a judgeship is one of the most highly esteemed positions in our society, and in this scenario, the judge is embracing the mental health practitioner as an extension of the judgeship.

Whenever there is the possibility of multiple roles, even if created by a judge, the mental health practitioner must always remember that law and professional ethics and standards proscribe conflicts of interests and inappropriate dual relations. Although it is feasible that the mental health practitioner could perform in multiple roles, it is best to exercise conservatism, and request that the judge make other arrangements. In so doing, the mental health practitioner is promoting quality services for the parents and children (and society), and minimizing the possibility of ethical, regulatory, or legal complaints later on, should one (or both) of the parents become dissatisfied with the outcome of the child custody legal proceedings.

In a similar vein, often the court or parents may ask a mental health practitioner who has provided treatment to one or both of the parents and/or the child to move into the role of custody evaluator. Here again, the multiple roles would present an affront to law and professional ethics and standards, and refusal of the multiple roles will contribute to quality care and risk management.

It is potentially possible for a mental health practitioner to provide testimony based on treatment, and for the testimony to have certain evaluative effects. When this occurs, the mental health practitioner should not, however, present the treatment-based information as a child custody evaluation. It should only be presented as treatment-based information that may assist the judge or another mental health practitioner who does a comprehensive custody evaluation to deal with the evaluative issues.

Further, it is deemed inappropriate for the mental health practitioner performing treatment or assessment roles to become a mediator, just as it is likely inappropriate for the mental health practitioner who has given expert testimony based on a custody evaluation to provide treatment to either or both of the parents and/or child later on. In later chapters, more will be said about multiple roles, and the proscription created by the law (at least in some jurisdictions) and professional ethics and standards.

 ➡ *Guideline:* *The mental health practitioner should have a clear and singular role in a child custody case; stated differently, multiple roles, even if requested by the court or the parents, should be opposed, and if insisted upon, a motion to withdraw from the case should be submitted to the court.*

AVOIDING TESTIMONY ABOUT LEGAL ISSUES

While there are jurisdictions that allow nonattorneys to serve as guardians, the issues are often so legal in nature that the most appropriate guardian for the child's legal interests (e.g., to promote the best interests of the child from a legal perspective) will be an attorney. In child custody cases, the mental health practitioner will often encounter legal issues that should not be addressed, except by someone with formal legal training and competency.

When offering testimony from the vantage point of having been a therapist, evaluator, or mediator, the mental health practitioner may be tempted or requested (by the parents, attorneys, or judge) to address legal issues in an authoritative manner, even while lacking professional training and competency to do so. These temptations and requests must be denied.

→ *Guideline: If the mental health practitioner is tempted or requested to address legal issues, care should be taken to avoid opinions, recommendations, or judgments for which the mental health practitioner lacks professional training and competency.*

PROCEDURAL RULES

The judicial system operates according to procedural rules. Evidence will be admissible only if it satisfies certain standards, commonly set forth in the so-called "Rules of Evidence," and in the case of child custody, "Rules of Civil Procedure." Most basically, the information submitted for admission must be relevant and material to the justiciable issues, that is, the questions put before the court (e.g., which parent should have custody).

In brief, the evidence is supposed to assist the trier of fact, the judge, in deciding what is in the best interests of the child:

In making a custody decision . . . the judge looks to the future in an attempt to discern whether the mother or the father will be the better parent. Further, custody adjudication focuses on the personal qualities of the parents. Each parent's efforts to persuade the judge that he or she is the better custodian may involve presenting evidence about the character, habits, life-style, and moral fitness of the former spouse. While in theory only evidence relating to an individual's capacity as a parent is relevant, any character deficiency or behavior that the judge is likely to view negatively often will be exposed. . . . In fact, no other form of litigation involves the same broad inquiry into the quality of an individual's character as does a custody dispute. (Scott & Emery, 1987, p. 27)

Therefore, the judge is the gatekeeper of the information that will be presented by, among others, the mental health professionals.

It is not unusual for a mental health practitioner to believe that certain information should be included in testimony about the case, only to find that the attorney for one of the parents will attempt to keep it from being expressed. Since the attorneys ask questions, and the mental health practitioner is presumably restricted to providing answers, there may not be an opportunity for the mental health practitioner to put forth certain information, notwithstanding the seeming importance for the best interests of the child specifically or the postdivorce mental health of the family in general.

→ **Guideline:** *The mental health practitioner should be familiar with procedural and evidentiary rules, as pertain to mental health testimony, and abide fully by them.*

THE BEST INTERESTS OF THE CHILD

For about three decades, family law has established that the best interests of the child is the prevailing criterion for custody-related determinations. Although the statutory language varies between jurisdictions to some extent (and, of course, judicial discretion can also create distinctions), there is general agreement about the definition of or what constitutes the best interests of the child:

> Currently, the best interests of the child is the governing standard in virtually all child custody disputes between natural parents arising within the fifty states. Some states have also specified factors focusing on the needs of the child whose custody is subject to dispute or on the parental factors that will affect the child's best interests that a judge can use when applying the standard. The criteria vary in form and application from state to state and often from court to court within the same jurisdiction. (Rohman et al., 1987, pp. 62-63)

Although there is general agreement, the concept of the best interests of the child is not as specific as one might think or prefer. While criteria for determining the best interests of the child (which will be discussed later) are contained in statutes, each jurisdiction (e.g., a particular state's laws) has latitude for: how each of the criteria is defined (e.g., for a given criterion); what evidence is necessary and how it will be weighted; appropriate judicial discretion (e.g., whether the trial judge's rulings on admissibility or weight on evidence was appropriate or erroneous); and whether the best interests of the child should be determined by here-and-now conditions or what will potentially be the situation in the future.

Since the early 1970s, the best interests of the child has been the criterion for judicial decision making. The initiation came when the National Conference of Commissioner on Uniform State Laws (1971), at its Annual Meeting in St. Louis in 1970, endorsed the Uniform Marriage and Divorce Act (UMDA); it provides five criteria for establishing the best interests of the child:

1. The wishes of the child's parent or parents as to his custody
2. The wishes of the child as to his custodian
3. The interaction and interrelationship of the child with his parent, his siblings, and any other person who may significantly affect the child's best interests
4. The child's adjustment to his home, school, and community
5. The mental and physical health of all individuals involved (Section 402; see Nurcombe & Partlett, 1994, p. 92)

The commitment to the best interests of the child received immediate and profound recognition, and states began to adopt, wholly or in part, the UMDA criteria.

As an example of a statute based on the best interests of the child, consider the following from the State of Michigan:

(a) The love, affection, and other emotional ties existing between the parties involved with the child.
(b) The capacity and disposition of the parties involved to give the child love, affection, and guidance and to continue the education and raising of the child in his or her religion or creed, if any.
(c) The capacity and disposition of the parties involved to provide the child with food, clothing, medical care or other remedial care recognized and permitted under the laws of this state in place of medical care, and other material needs.
(d) The length of time the child has lived in a stable, satisfactory environment, and the desirability of maintaining continuity.

(e) The permanence, as a family unit, of the existing or proposed custodial home or homes.
(f) The moral fitness of the parties involved.
(g) The mental and physical health of the parties involved.
(h) The home, school, and community record of the child.
(i) The reasonable preference of the child, if the court deems the child to be of sufficient age to express preference.
(j) The willingness and ability of each of the parties to facilitate and encourage a close and continuing parent-child relationship between the child and the other parent or the child and the parents.
(k) Domestic violence, regardless of whether the violence was directed against or witnessed by the child.
(l) Any other factor considered by the court to be relevant to a particular child custody dispute. (Michigan Child Custody Act, MCLA § 722.23)

Incidentally, Michigan was one of the first states to adopt legislation to codify the best interests of the child, and continues to promote changes (e.g., sections j and k of MCLA § 722.23).

The psychological nature of the best interests of the child has received considerable professional advocacy. J. Goldstein, Freud, and Solnit (1973) state that:

- Placement decisions should safeguard the child's need for continuity of relationships. (p. 31)
- Placement decisions should reflect the child's, not the adult's, sense of time. (p. 40)
- Child placement decisions must take into account the law's incapacity to supervise interpersonal relationships and the limits of knowledge to make long-range predictions. (p. 49)

Perhaps the most controversial aspect of the position taken by J. Goldstein, Freud, and Solnit was the assertion that the best interests of the child could potentially be met by other than biological parents, namely psychological parents (e.g., other relatives, friends, etc.).

In the mid-1970s, I reviewed statutory and case law, and identified 20 primary factors that appeared to be present in child custody decision making (Woody, 1975, 1977a). With feedback from lawyers, psychiatrists, psychologists, and social workers, the factors were ranked for importance; although there were some differences between rankings for mothers versus fathers, connoting possible sexism (Woody, 1977c), the rankings for the factors were:

1. Quality of relationship with the child
2. Mental health
3. Child-rearing attitudes of the parents
4. Child-care history
5. Personal behavior
6. Physical health
7. Personality
8. General life history
9. Morality
10. Intelligence
11. Criminal record
12. Knowledge of child development
13. Income
14. Stability of residence
15. Aspirations
16. Education
17. Age
18. Sexual behavior
19. Religion
20. Vocation
    (For additional information see Woody, 1977a, 1977b, 1977c, 1978.)

The legal onus was placed on the parents to establish, such as in custody evaluations conducted by mental health professionals, that they could, in fact, meet the best interests of the child.

As discussed in other chapters, the support for the best interests of the child has led to statutory and judicial recognition of keeping both parents involved with the child, that is, not allowing the concept of a sole residential custodial parent to lessen the involvement of the other parent. This emphasis is, of course, in accord with a fundamental premise of this book.

Using terms like "joint custody" and "shared parental responsibility," legislators and judges have promoted both parents' having a continuing role in the decision making for their child. For example, consider the Florida statute that defines shared parental responsibility:

> For purposes of shared parental responsibility and primary residence, the best interests of the child shall include an evaluation of all factors affecting the welfare and interests of the child, including, but not limited to:
>
> (a) The parent who is most likely to allow the child frequent and continuing contact with the nonresidential parent.
> (b) The love, affection, and other emotional ties existing between the parents and the child.
> (c) The capacity and disposition of the parents to provide the child with food, clothing, medical care or other remedial care recognized and permitted under the laws of this state in lieu of medical care, and other material needs.
> (d) The length of time the child has lived in a stable, satisfactory environment and the desirability of maintaining continuity.
> (e) The permanence, as a family unit, of the existing or proposed custodial home.
> (f) The moral fitness of the parents.
> (g) The mental and physical health of the parents.
> (h) The home, school, and community record of the child.
> (i) The reasonable preference of the child, if the court deems the child to be of sufficient intelligence, understanding, and experience to express a preference.
> (j) The willingness and ability of each parent to facilitate and encourage a close and continuing parent-child relationship between the child and the other parent.
> (k) Evidence that any party has knowingly provided false information to the court regarding a domestic violation proceeding. . . .
> (l) Evidence of domestic violence or child abuse.
> (m) Any other fact considered by the court to be relevant. (Florida Statute 61.13 [3])

Of particular interest, this statute weights parental cooperation for facilitating parent-child relations, as well as false information and actual conduct relevant to domestic violence and child abuse (as will be discussed in the next section). Also, current statutes commonly disavow a presumption that the gender of the parent per se will determine the best interests of the child.

Florida law also honors the best interests of the child when a primary residential parent wishes to relocate the child. Even though the move may materially affect the visitation schedule and access of the secondary parent, the court *must* consider the following factors:

1. Whether the move would be likely to improve the general quality of life for both the residential parent and the child.
2. The extent to which visitation rights have been allowed and exercised.
3. Whether the primary residential parent, once out of the jurisdiction, will be likely to comply with any substitute visitation arrangements.
4. Whether the substitute visitation will be adequate to foster a continuing meaningful relationship between the child and the secondary residential parent.
5. Whether the cost of transportation is financially affordable by one or both parties.
6. Whether the move is in the best interests of the child. (Florida Statute 61.13 [3] [d]).

In conclusion, there is no doubt that the best interests of the child constitutes the foremost criterion for child custody evaluations, interventions, and testimony. Every mental health practitioner should be fully versed in the child custody laws for his or her jurisdiction. (For a compilation of family law legislation, see Wadlington [1995].)

CHILD ABUSE AND NEGLECT

In child custody cases, allegations of abuse or neglect receive careful scrutiny by all concerned. As mentioned in the preceding section, some state statutes, such as in Florida, give abuse specific emphasis. From experience, it seems that, with or without legislative specificity per se, there is profound awareness by the judiciary of domestic violence in general and child abuse and neglect in specific.

In today's society, abuse and neglect of children has reached epidemic proportions: "Conservative estimates indicate that almost two thousand infants and young children die from abuse and neglect by parents or caretakers each year, or five children every day . . . [and] abuse and neglect kills 5.4 out of every 100,000 children age four and under" (Committee on Professional Practice and Standards, 1998, p. 2). From a survey of research relevant to the connection of abuse to psychopathology, Read (1997) concludes that child abuse leads to long-term negative effects, including: "depression, susceptibility to suicide, anxiety disorders, eating disorders, sexual dysfunction, dissociative disorders, personality disorders, posttraumatic stress disorder (PTSD), and substance abuse" (p. 448). All states have mandatory reporting laws (albeit that there are differences), which means that the mental health practitioner must be prepared to fulfill the duty to reveal information about suspected or admitted/observed child abuse or neglect to the relevant children's protective service.

➔ *Guideline: The prevalence of child abuse and neglect is so great and the consequences so severe that the mental health practitioner should deliberately, but cautiously, explore this issue in every child custody case.*

Providing expert testimony about possible child abuse and neglect presents profound problems. First, the quest to protect children must be tempered by honoring the legal rights of the person(s) accused of having abused or neglected a child. Second, evaluation of abuse and neglect situations is plagued with unreliable indicators and information. Third, mental health practitioners will encounter inappropriate requests, such as from attorneys and judges, to opine about child abuse and neglect. If any of these three issues is handled poorly or incorrectly, the result could be an ethical, regulatory, or legal complaint against the mental health practitioner.

Any notion that a child will not provide a false allegation about abuse is ill-founded: "Research examining child sexual abuse has yet to provide accurate numbers on child victims or definitive markers that differentiate true cases of child sexual abuse from those cases that are not true" (Kuehnle, 1996, p. 1). Well-designed research studies have produced, however, convincing evidence that

18 a child's memory and perception can, in fact, be altered and shaped by messages or conditions imposed by others (Oldershaw & Bagby, 1997).

There is also reason to believe that some parents, particularly when embroiled in a divorce or custody dispute, are motivated to alienate the child from the other parent and resort, consciously or unconsciously, to brainwashing the child (Oldershaw & Bagby, 1997). Due to the "parental alienation syndrome," the courts are now suspicious of virtually every allegation of abuse or neglect that surfaces, particularly for the first time, during a divorce or custody legal proceeding. As Ross (1999) describes it: "What is particularly problematic for courts is the data, which state that children are susceptible to adult influences and may tender false allegations based on an adult interviewer's conscious or subconscious cues or misunderstanding of the events; or, in difficult divorce situations, the child's articulations may be influenced by a histrionic or vindictive emotional response of one parent toward the other" (p. 33).

The evaluation of possible child abuse and neglect must be conducted in a manner that avoids creating undue stress or trauma for the child, and guards against suggestions from the mental health practitioner tainting the information: "In the past decade, there has been an exponential increase in research on the accuracy of young children's memories and degree to which young children's memories and reports can be molded by suggestions implanted by adult interviewers" (Ross, 1999, p. 33).

Working with child abuse and neglect issues cannot be left to chance. The prudent mental health practitioner should make a special effort to cultivate the knowledge and skills necessary to deal effectively with child abuse and neglect. Kuehnle (1996) provides an encyclopedic-like source for conducting child abuse and neglect evaluations, and a useful summary of treatment issues for child sexual abuse in particular (Kuehnle, 1998). Every mental health practitioner should be familiar with, among other sources, *Guidelines for Psychological Evaluations in Child Protection Matters* (Committee on Professional Practice and Standards, 1998).

➤ *Guideline: The mental health practitioner should tailor the strategies for evaluating the possibility or effects of child abuse and neglect to avoid unnecessary stress for or contaminating suggestions to the child.*

➜ *Guideline: The testimony by the mental health practitioner should be framed by the research on a child's memory and suggestibility, and rely on systematic data collection that includes reliable and objective measures.*

For both quality care and risk management, how the mental health practitioner deals with the ultimate legal question is paramount in importance. Stated bluntly, unless the mental health practitioner was in the room when the child abuse or neglect occurred, there is no way of knowing with a reasonable degree of scholarly or behavioral science certainty that the child abuse or neglect did, in fact, occur. Granted, if the alleged perpetrator admitted the child abuse or neglect or if a credible witness (or several witnesses) observed the child abuse or neglect when it happened, the report would be convincing. On the other hand, these witnesses could and should testify themselves in the child custody, abuse, or neglect legal proceedings. If the admissions or observations were reported to the mental health practitioner, he or she could potentially testify accordingly, unless the court deemed it inadmissible because of hearsay. However, the ultimate legal question, "Did or did not the abuse or neglect occur?" is for the judge (or jury) to answer.

Public policy and law have not endowed mental health practitioners with a special license to investigate and decide abuse and neglect matters. States have, of course, established children's protective services (CPS) for this duty, and granted special rights, privileges, and immunity to responsible CPS workers. Unless employed by a CPS agency, the mental health practitioner cannot serve as a substitute.

➜ *Guideline: If the mental health practitioner is asked to use inductive or deductive reasoning and opine whether the alleged child abuse did or did not occur, the mental health practitioner should respectfully decline to answer due to a lack of scholarly or behavioral science basis.*

In distinguishing why the judge (or jury), but not the mental health practitioner, should answer the ultimate legal question, it is simply a matter of the public policy and legal definitions for the respective roles. A judge has been designated to be the trier of fact, that is, to decide what merits consideration in a legal decision and what should be the decision; and the judge is granted immunity from a retaliatory legal action. On the contrary, the mental health practitioner has been designated to provide information, based on professional training and experiences, that will assist the trier of fact. While the mental health practitioner can address the ultimate legal question (and in some jurisdictions, offer an answer), there is no assured immunity from a retaliatory legal action. Also, there are many ultimate legal questions that would require an answer that lacks an adequate scholarly or behavioral science basis; thus, an answer by the mental health practitioner would be potentially a breech of professionalism.

On the matter of immunity from legal action, mandatory reporting of possible child abuse to a state children's protective service is present in all jurisdictions; and it is common to specify that a report will be immune from suit. Nonetheless, I have provided legal representation to mental health practitioners who have, in fact, been sued for making good faith reports of suspected child abuse or neglect. In each instance, the report was simply a matter-of-fact (nonadvocacy) statement to the particular children's protection service. In one case, the alleged perpetrator filed a lawsuit against the mental health practitioner for not warning him beforehand that his admission of a long-term incestuous relationship was subject to mandatory reporting to the children's protective service. In another case, the mental health practitioner made a report of a child's comments about possible abuse. The alleged perpetrator filed a lawsuit, claiming defamation and mental distress due to the mental health practitioner's not having a reasonable basis for the report to the children's protective service, which he claimed was verified by the dismissal of the investigation by the children's protective service. In each of these cases—and despite the mandated reporting, matter-of-fact communication (nonadvocacy), and presumed immunity—the respective court involved would not dismiss the retaliatory lawsuit by summary judgment until many months after it was filed. In the meantime, the well-intentioned mental health practitioner suffered emotionally and financially.

➔ *Guideline: Because the law requires mandatory reporting of suspected child abuse and neglect, but immunity is not assured, the mental health practitioner should be familiar with the governing laws and practices, cautiously investigate and document the information about the possibility of child abuse or neglect,*

and assiduously adhere to being simply a reporter, not an advo-
cate of whether the alleged child abuse or neglect did or did not
occur.

Finally, addressing the possibility of child abuse and neglect is in accord with the best interests of the child and is, therefore, important to consider in child custody testimony, including in an evaluation. It is clear, however, that the prudent mental health practitioner must exercise extreme caution when dealing with this subject.

DEVELOPMENTAL CONSIDERATIONS

Relying on developmental theory, the prevailing definition of the best interests of the child places heavy emphasis on continuity of relationships. The divorce process threatens to disrupt the child's contacts with parents (who will be living separately), siblings (who may be divided between the parents), extended family members (who will most likely support the blood-related parent more than the other parent), and neighborhood friends (especially if the child is forced to move). Worse yet, the divorce commonly tests, and could weaken, the child's affective bonds to and trust of one or both parents. When a parent engages in efforts to alienate the child from the other parent, the potential for harm is increased. If the child's development is to be safeguarded, the foregoing conditions must be opposed: "Thus continuity is a guideline because emotional attachments are tenuous and vulnerable in early life, and children need stability of relationships for their healthy growth and development" (J. Goldstein et al., 1996, p. 20).

➔ *Guideline: At all times, the mental health practitioner should promote positive conditions to further the child's healthy development, guarding against and counteracting destructive or harmful influences from either or both parents.*

If there is a dispute over child custody or visitation arrangements, the parents tend to conceptualize the best interests of the child according to how much creature-comfort and personal contact time each parent can provide. Often the creature-comfort factor emphasizes financial support and material acquisitions, such as toys, and the personal contact time is determined quantitatively, rather than qualitatively. While indefensible by psychological theory, this illogical view is understandable: "Since continuity may not play as significant a role in later life, its importance may be underrated by adult decision-makers" (J. Goldstein et al., 1996, p. 19).

→ *Guideline: In a nonjudgmental manner, the mental health practitioner should educate both parents about the psychological implications of the criteria about which the mental health practitioner will testify and that the court will use in determining the best interests of the child.*

In keeping with their developmental framework, J. Goldstein et al. (1996) believe that any placement decision should consider the child's sense of time (e.g., the need for immediate gratification and security). They also encourage the court to recognize the fallibility of its long-range predictions and inability to manage family relationships.

→ *Guideline: While the cognitive social-learning and family systems approaches support consideration of future conditions in the child's family system, the mental health practitioner should readily admit the fallibility of prognostications, notwithstanding certain scholarly and behavioral science underpinnings.*

Finally, rather than presuming that only biological parents can meet the best interests of the child, Goldstein et al. say: "We propose that the placement standard should be one that provides the *least detrimental available alternative for safeguarding a child's growth and development*" (p. 50). The latter means that a biological-parent status alone does not determine the placement decision. Rather, their view is that the judicial determination should look to anyone available to be the "psychological parent" who will provide the "least detrimental alternative" to the child.

→ *Guideline: Although the natural parents will usually receive deference from the court (unless there is evidence of abuse or neglect), the mental health practitioner should address the psychological bonding between the child and any adult who has standing to seek custody or visitation rights.*

The issues presented in the foregoing paragraphs are controversial. Therefore, if the mental health practitioner is asked to opine about any of these matters, care should be taken to restrict opinions to those that have a scholarly and behavioral science basis, and present the opinions in a tactful manner. Not only could the parents be offended by opinions about, say, the least detrimental alternative, the court could be offended by being challenged on its fallibility to forecast what is best for the children. Any negative reaction by the parents or the court raises the possibility of ethical, regulatory, or legal complaints against the mental health practitioner.

THE PREFERENCES OF JUDGES

Judges seem to reflect concern about healthy and optimal development of the child through attributing great importance to continuity of living in general and residence in specific for the child. One judge commented, "I want that child to continue sleeping in the same bedroom and walk the same route to school, regardless of which parent is watching television in the living room." Combining the principles of continuity of relationships and environmental stability (e.g., avoiding disruption of established life-routines, such as playmates), the judge may use this principle to assign custody to the parent who will remain in the same house where the child has been living.

There is too little known to generalize about the preferences of judges. In one survey, however, Lowery (1981) found that the most significant factors (in order of preference) for judges were: parental mental instability; the parent's sense of responsibility for the child; kinship ties; parental moral character; the capacity to provide stability; the parent's affection for the child; the desirability of keeping siblings together; the capacity to provide access to schools; the child's tender years; and parental physical health. With all due respect to Lowery, this survey had a limited sample to start with and is likely outdated. Therefore, it seems more prudent to believe that the preferences of judges are much more aligned with the laws of a particular jurisdiction, filtered through, of course, judicial discretion.

The statutes and appellate cases in the jurisdiction in which the court is located will construct the criteria for determining the best interests of the child. Of course, judicial discretion will have an explicit or implicit role in the decisions. For example, one judge is known to almost always inquire about the religious convictions of each parent, while another judge almost always asks about the importance of siblings staying together.

→ **Guideline:** *The mental health practitioner should recognize and accept that the criteria for the best interests of the child may vary between jurisdictions, and that the laws will be filtered through the judge's personal preferences.*

THE PREFERENCES OF THE CHILD

At one time, children were kept away from the custody proceedings. The idea was two-fold. First, the reasoning was that children should not suffer the negative consequences of seeing and hearing the parents acting as adversaries. Second, it was believed that children were incapable of giving meaningful testimony.

The law is always fluid and evolving, and views about the child's preferences have changed. At present, favor rests with allowing a child to give information and express an opinion to the court: "Although in some quarters the direct involvement of children in matters pertaining to their family remains controversial, the conventional wisdom now seems to be that children's voices ought to be heard, at least when the child is beyond the infant stage" (Melton et al., 1997, p. 498).

Since public policies and laws require that the child custody legal proceeding be predicated on the best interests of the child, it is logical that the child's views about with whom he or she would like to reside should, under some conditions, be considered. Today, the law provides definite procedural accommodation for considering the wishes of the child, although jurisdictions vary on this matter.

As will be discussed, there is no single standard or practice for involving a child in the proceeding, but in accord with the Uniform Marriage and Divorce Act, judicial consideration can be given to the wishes of the children. Indeed, at the present time, "every state explicitly includes this factor for judicial consideration in contested custody cases either through statutory or common law" (Crosby-Currie, 1996, p. 289).

The jurisdictions differ about when a child's testimony will be allowed and how it will be weighted. Slicker (1998) opposes any inflexible approach, but endorses, upon motion to the court, a judge's questioning the child:

The judge should determine that: 1) the child is intellectually and emotionally mature enough to have a valid opinion (probably at least six years of age; 2) the child knows the difference between truth and lies; 3) the child has an opinion on the issue before the court; 4) the child wants to voice his or her opinion (no child should be forced to make a choice between his or her parents if he or she does not want to); and 5) the child is not being threatened or bribed by someone to give a false opinion. (p. 48)

➔ *Guideline: The mental health practitioner should be prepared to offer testimony based on scholarly and behavioral science information about how to evaluate the elements of a child's preferences.*

From research on evaluating eyewitness testimony, Goodman and Hahn (1987) provide information that has application to a child's testifying about his or her preferences for custody and visitation:

> If children are questioned properly, their errors are usually those of omission rather than commission—that is, children tend to omit details or refuse to answer but are unlikely to invent things that never happened. . . . To the extent that children are more suggestible than adults, it is essential that interviewers avoid asking leading questions of them. Even if the child does not accept the suggestion, attorneys can use the fact that suggestive questioning was employed to discredit perfectly accurate testimony. (p. 278)

The suggestibility of the child is of paramount importance, especially when an allegation of parental alienation syndrome is presented.

➔ *Guideline: The mental health practitioner should be skilled at eliciting information relevant to the child's preference, without shaping or suggesting the nature of the child's communications or preferences; and, if needed, pursue special training for these professional functions.*

Judges differ considerably in their willingness or desire to hear a child's preference about custody or visitation, and how the information should be obtained (Crosby-Currie, 1996). The differences seem to be more idiosyncratic to the judge's personal values and beliefs, rather than based on demographic or legal factors per se.

→ *Guideline: Unless deemed proper by the designated role definition for the particular child custody case, the mental health practitioner should not advocate a child's testifying; but the mental health practitioner may, if role-appropriate, inform the court about the possible usefulness of the child's preferences for the court's decision making.*

If the child's views are to be expressed, the court commonly wants assurance, such as from a mental health practitioner or an attorney, that the child has sufficient maturation (intellectually and socially) to offer useful information, such as expressing a reasonable opinion that does, in fact, address issues pertaining to the best interests of the child. This is not to say, however, that the mental health practitioner will necessarily be the solicitor and/or evaluator of the wishes of the child. More will be said on this matter shortly.

If a child is to be involved in the proceedings, the judge must rule on whether the child will appear in open court or in the judge's chambers. Being in the judge's chambers (offices), instead of the courtroom, is intended to take some of the pressure off the child, as well as avoiding the courtroom which might have nonfamily members in attendance.

While it can be argued that the parents and their legal counsel have a right to be present when any evidence is presented to the court (and indeed, cross-examine the witness), including what is said by the child about his or her preferences for child custody or visitation, sometimes the parents are pressed by the court or attorneys to not be present. Likewise, some judges will even press the attorneys to not be present. When a judge interviews a child there are often violations of due process (Rogers, 1987): "Although the judges are acting to protect the children, the due process limitations of many in-chambers interviews is a clear abrogation of the parents' right to hear and respond to all the evidence used to make a judicial determination" (Crosby-Currie, 1996, p. 292).

Depending on the circumstances, the child may be interviewed formally (the attorneys may examine and cross-examine the child). Whether in the courtroom or the judge's chambers, the judge can also ask questions. It is not unusual for the judge to shift into a "grandparent-like" persona.

One judge routinely has young children sit on his lap as he talks to the child about what happens between the child and each of the parents and other family members. This same judge also prefers to hold the interviews in his office and to exclude the parents, and sternly advises the attorneys to sit quietly and unobtrusively in the back of the room. He sometimes requests that the mental health practitioner(s) also observe, which might, of course, shape the subsequent testimony by the mental health practitioner.

Although often done with reservations, most judges are willing to hear a child's information and opinion. Scott, Reppucci, and Aber (1988) states:

> The judges reported that children below the age of six were the subject of fifty percent of litigated custody disputes, and most agreed that children's wishes in this age group were irrelevant to the decision. In contrast, the vast majority of judges reported that they routinely attempted in some way to get information about older children's wishes. Even for children in the six- to nine-year age group, sixty-five percent of judges tried to obtain some information about the child's preference, although usually not directly from the child. For children over fourteen years of age, ninety-seven percent of judges considered the child's views. (pp. 1046-1047)

In considering this report, Melton et al. (1997) speculate: "The judges' behavior may have been based as much on practical considerations as it was on respect for older children's opinions" (p. 498). That is, the child who feels a part of the decision making is most apt to adhere to the orders issued by the court.

➜ *Guideline: Unless requested specifically for input, the mental health practitioner should not critique the judge's views about child testimony or elicitation of the child's preferences or opinions; it would be potentially improper for the mental health practitioner to suborn criticism of the judge's activities.*

It seems that the older the child, the greater the weight given to his or her information and preferences; and being over the age of 12 tends to lead to more importance being given to the child's preferences (Scott et al., 1988; Settle & Lowery, 1982). "Overall, the literature suggests that at about 6 to 8 years of age, children are sometimes involved, and at about 12 to 14 years of age, children are almost always involved" (Crosby-Currie, 1996, p. 292). Further, from a survey of judges, attorneys, and mental health professionals, Crosby-Currie concludes:

> That age mediates the weight as well as the asking of children's wishes. All groups reported that children under 8 were not likely to be asked about their wishes but children 14 and older were reported by all groups as being likely to be asked. In addition, the wishes of children 11 and under were given at most moderate weight, whereas the wishes of 16- and 17-year-olds were given a great deal of weight. This finding is particularly interesting given that, although the laws of none of the states surveyed vests the wishes of an older child with controlling weight, in practical terms these wishes may be determinative in a substantial proportion of contested cases. (p. 305)

The survey finding supports that mental health practitioners should be involved in evaluating the preferences of a child relevant to child custody issues.

The apparent option to the judge eliciting the child's preference would be for the preferences of the child to be included in the custody evaluation conducted by a mental health practitioner. This choice may, however, be opposed by the court:

> Mental health professionals generally agreed with the idea that they, not the judge, should conduct interviews of children in contested custody cases. Judges on the other hand, were very unlikely to agree with this idea. (Crosby-Currie, 1996, p. 307)

This issue holds the potential for conflict between the mental health practitioner and the court.

Regardless of the importance attributed to weighting the wishes of the child, judicial discretion prevails. Regardless of the child's chronological age, the judge who believes that the child lacks adequate intellectual and social reasoning and/or harbors dubious motives will attribute minimal importance to the child's preferences. On the other hand, judges often make comments like, "Once a child becomes a teenager and has his or her mind set on a certain custody or visitation preference, there is little the court can do to require otherwise." As Melton et al. (1997) put it: "If a fifteen-year-old is refusing to live with one parent but not the other, the law may have few means (short of draconian measures) to enforce an order to grant custody to the parent with whom the adolescent is in conflict" (p. 498).

➜ *Guideline: The mental health practitioner should request and clarify judicial preferences about exploration of the child's preferences; and if there is disagreement about whether an exploration should occur or who should conduct the exploration, the mental health practitioner should present a reasoned viewpoint to the court and abide by and support the judicial decision that ensues.*

➜ *Guideline: If the mental health practitioner is designated to explore the child's preferences for custody and visitation, the evaluation should recognize the likely importance of the age and maturity factors and deal with the intellectual, social reasoning, and logic factors that underlie the child's preferences.*

THE PREFERENCES OF MENTAL HEALTH PRACTITIONERS

Since the mental health practitioner is not the trier of fact and not a party of the action per se, there is little or no room for advocacy of preferences. That is, the mental health practitioner has the role of offering scholarly and behavioral science information to the trier of fact. The parents and the child hold the right to express personal opinions. Nonetheless, personal (nonprofessional) opinions and preferences commonly creep into testimony from mental health practitioners.

Earlier in this chapter, I mentioned a nationwide survey of lawyers, psychiatrists, psychologists, and social workers that I conducted (Woody, 1975, 1977a, 1977b, 1977c, 1978) on the criteria used for child custody. It was found that the views about the best interests of the child were sometimes subject to influence from the professional's gender and discipline. Overall, the professionals did not differ significantly in the importance attributed to various decision-making factors between the mother and the father; and the professionals' demographic variables correlated with evaluative stance. It was clear that the professionals considered certain factors to be more important than others, although the priority might not have legal authority or behavioral science basis. As a reminder, the five highest ranked factors for both the mother and the father were: quality of relationship with the child; mental health; child-rearing attitudes of the parents; child-care history; and personal behavior.

More recently, preferences from mental health practitioners are evident in the "Guidelines for Child Custody Evaluations in Divorce Proceedings" promulgated by the American Psychological Association (APA; 1994). It should be noted that these guidelines are aspirational and intended for psychologists. It would seem, however, that these guidelines can be generalized and applied to all of the mental health disciplines.

These child custody guidelines from the American Psychological Association (1994) reflect much of what has already been said. Child custody evaluations should be framed by the best interests of the child: "The child's interests and well-being are paramount" (p. 677). The primary focus should be on the parents' capacity to meet the child's psychological needs: "(a) an assessment of the adults' capacities for parenting, including whatever knowledge, attributes, skills, and abilities, or lack thereof, are present; (b) an assessment of the psychological functioning and developmental needs of each child and of the wishes of each child where appropriate; and (c) an assessment of the functional ability of each parent to meet these needs, including an evaluation of the interaction between each adult and child" (p. 678). Also: "Psychopathology may be relevant to such an assessment, insofar as it has impact on the child or the ability to parent, but it is not the primary focus" (p. 678).

In keeping with earlier statements about the mental health practitioner's not being a trier of fact, these child custody guidelines promote objectivity and impartiality:

> The psychologist does not act as a judge, who makes the ultimate decision applying the law to all relevant evidence. Neither does the psychologist act as an advocating attorney, who strives to present his or her client's best possible case. (APA, 1994, p. 678)

Also, if impartiality cannot be accepted by others involved in the case or maintained by the psychologist, "the psychologist should consider withdrawing from the case" (p. 678).

Preferences are also evident in the specialized competency that is deemed essential for custody evaluations. That is, competence in psychological assessments, "is necessary, but not sufficient" (p. 678). The mental health practitioner must understand the nature of the client (e.g., a young child), child and family development and psychopathology, and the effects of divorce and be familiar "with applicable legal standards and procedures, including laws governing divorce and custody adjudications in his or her state or jurisdiction" (p. 678). The latter should include laws on child abuse, neglect, and family violence. Also important is "current knowledge of scientific and professional developments" (p. 678).

→ *Guideline: When testifying in child custody cases, the mental health practitioner should conform to the "Guidelines for Child Custody Evaluations in Divorce Proceedings" promulgated by the American Psychological Association (1994), which means that the mental health practitioner will maintain objectivity (i.e., opine according to a scholarly and behavioral science basis) and impartiality (i.e., nonadvocacy); and carefully evaluate the best interests of the child, individual and family development and psychopathology, and the parents' capacity to meet the child's psychological needs.*

Chapter 6

ESTABLISHING ROLE AND FUNCTIONS

In every professional activity, the mental health practitioner must be cognizant of and accommodate the laws and professional ethics and standards that pertain to the particular service. Weithorn (1987) characterizes involvement in child custody proceedings as an ethical "minefield," and warns: "And yet despite the plethora of ethical pitfalls that characterize any divorce custody evaluation under the best of conditions, psychologists are not relieved from the responsibility to uphold the highest standards of their profession" (p. 206). This chapter will present information to help the mental health practitioner define and maintain a proper role and functions, as will lead to testimony that yields quality service and risk management.

PRESCRIPTIONS AND PROSCRIPTIONS FROM THE COURT

Throughout the earlier chapters, the discussion has revealed: the potential discrepancy in roles and goals of attorneys and mental health practitioners; the risk that can occur by a poorly conceptualized involvement in child custody legal proceedings; and the need to provide mental health services that are in accord with the law, professional ethics and standards, and the preferences and orders of the court. Sometimes there will be conflicting views, preferences, and decisions, and the mental health practitioner must assiduously pursue resolution of these problems and, at all times, promote quality care and risk management.

Perhaps the ultimate safeguard of both quality care and risk management comes from the judge's specifying the mental health practitioner's role and functions. Stated differently, if the mental health practitioner provides services as specified and directed by the judge—which should be documented by a court order—it is likely that the quality of services will be high and that there will be an important shield from ethical, regulatory, and legal complaints. Unfortunately, even a judicial shield of this nature can be penetrated if the mental health practitioner lapses into malpractice.

→ *Guideline: It is wise for the mental health practitioner to seek judicial clarification for literally every aspect of the role and functions that the mental health practitioner considers or proposes for child custody services, and to have the judge's decisions document the role and functions specifically in a court order.*

The foregoing guideline is applicable to virtually all issues discussed in this book. Also, this guideline serves as an important transition to the topic of this chapter, namely case management and practice issues.

MAINTAINING A CLEAR AND SINGULAR ROLE

In child custody cases, there are five possible roles for the mental health practitioner:

1. Guardian *ad litem* for the child;
2. Treating therapist for the child, parents, or immediate family;
3. Evaluator of the individuals whose psychological characteristics are relevant and material to the child custody determination;
4. Mediator to resolve the dispute(s) between the parents without undue litigation;
5. Expert critic, who speaks in support of or in opposition to the testimony offered by other mental health practitioners (e.g., a treating therapist).

Entry into a child custody case should be predicated upon a clear and precise role definition, one that is in accord with laws and professional ethics and standards pertaining to the mental health practitioner. Ideally, the role, whatever it may be, should be set forth (as discussed previously) in specific detail and in a written court order, thereby supporting appropriate and high quality mental health services for all concerned and minimizing the possibility of ethical, regulatory, or legal complaints against the mental health practitioner. Whether by court order or accepted upon referral, the mental health practitioner should define (preferably in writing) the role and functions from the outset of professional services.

➔ *Guideline: The role for the mental health practitioner should be determined before professional services are provided. To increase acceptance of the role and eliminate subsequent misunderstanding, any relevant person should have an opportunity to respond to the role definition, and the decision should be in writing.*

Earlier, it was asserted that multiple roles should be avoided, no matter who requests the multiple roles or how skilled the mental health practitioner may be. Law and professional ethics and standards dictate that the mental health practitioner should be involved in a child custody case with a clear and singular role. The "Specialty Guidelines for Forensic Psychologists" (Committee on Ethical Guidelines for Forensic Psychologists, 1991) states: "For psychologists recognize potential conflicts of interest in dual relationships with parties to a legal proceeding, and they seek to minimize their effects" (p. 659). With that statement as precursor, consider the following from the "Guidelines for Child Custody Evaluations in Divorce Proceedings" (American Psychological Association, 1994):

> The psychologist avoids multiple relationships. Psychologists generally avoid conducting a child custody evaluation in a case in which the psychologist served in a therapeutic role for the child or his or her immediate family or had other involvement that may compromise the psychologist's objectivity. This should not, however, preclude the psychologist from testifying in the case as a fact witness concerning treatment of the child. In addition, during the course of a child custody evaluation, a psychologist does not accept any of the involved participants in the evaluation as a therapy client. Therapeutic contact with the child or in-

volved participants following a child custody evaluation is undertaken with caution. (p. 678)

Although the foregoing quotations are aspirational and intended for psychologists, they reflect what seems to be the prevailing contemporary notions about the involvement of any mental health practitioner, regardless of professional discipline, in a child custody case. In fact, some licensing boards have created rules accordingly. For example, the Florida Board of Psychology has the following rule:

It is a conflict of interest for a psychologist who has treated a minor or any of the adults involved in a custody or visitation action to perform a forensic evaluation for the purpose of recommending with which adult the minor should reside, which adult should have custody, or what visitation should be allowed. Consequently, a psychologist who treats a minor or any of the adults involved in a custody or visitation action may not also perform a forensic evaluation for custody, residence or visitation of the minor. This subsection does not limit a psychologist who treats a minor from providing a court or a mental health professional performing an evaluation with information about the minor from the psychologist's perspective as a treating psychologist, so long as the psychologist does not violate confidentiality. (Florida Administrative Code, Chapter 64B19-18.006)

Further, countless judges have issued negative opinions about a mental health practitioner's being in multiple roles.

Suspicion about and rejection of multiple roles is understandable. It would be easy for the mental health practitioner to consciously or unconsciously veer away from objectivity and impartiality.

This assertion is applicable to all roles and functions, regardless of the conditions in a particular child custody case. To do other than adhere strictly to a clear and singular role is to potentially violate professional ethics and standards, and possibly state statutes and rules. When this occurs, the mental health practitioner has jeopardized quality care and created a high risk of ethical, regulatory, and legal complaints.

Although the restriction to a single role may not be specifically addressed in the laws and rules for the jurisdiction in which the mental health practitioner provides services or in the ethics or position papers promulgated by professional associations with which the mental health practitioner is affiliated, common practice, case law, and other authoritative sources construct a "standard" that proscribes more than one role in a child custody case. Believing that there are special circumstances that would unquestionably justify multiple roles is foolish.

 ➡ **Guideline:** *The mental health practitioner should adhere to a clear and singular role in a child custody case.*

COMPETENCE AND THE STANDARD OF CARE

Competence is the foundation of fulfilling the requisite standard of care. There are several possible ways to define the standard of care that is applicable to any given child custody case. This lack of a sole definition creates a risk of violation. Granello and Witmer (1998) state: "*Standards of care* can be defined as the professional conduct practiced by reasonable and prudent practitioners who have special knowledge and ability for the diagnosis of treatment of clinical conditions" (pp. 371-372). Placed in the context of a child custody case, this definition would support the idea that the mental health practitioner must practice in accord with others who have "special knowledge and ability" for child custody matters. In other words, the degree of competence expected will be determined, in part, by other mental health practitioners who provide services to child custody cases.

Having scholarly and behavioral science bases for expert interpretations, opinions, and recommendations in child custody cases is fundamental to competence. According to Melton et al. (1997), the problems arising from mental health practitioners exceeding their expertise and using quasi-scientific data in child custody legal proceedings has led to unique professional ethics: "The most basic ethical issues for clinicians involved in custody disputes may be ones of monitoring the limits of competence and avoiding trespass across these limits" (p. 484). Similarly, Weithorn and Grisso (1987) align overreaching one's competence with a breach of ethics:

> A most serious problem in psychological testimony in custody cases is psychologists' failure to inform courts of the limitations of their evaluations. The shortcoming may re-

sult from the temptation to speak with authority, the pressures of the adversarial system, or psychologists' failure to appreciate that they are "overreaching." Whatever the reason, failure to use caution in one's statements violates ethical principles and notions of what constitutes competent psychological practice. (p. 178)

They emphasize that "the parties . . . deserve from psychologists the utmost in conscientiousness and humility" (p. 178).

➡ *Guideline: The mental health practitioner should have training and preparation for providing child custody services with a degree of competence appropriate to law and professional ethics and standards, and comparable to the qualifications of other mental health practitioners providing services to child custody cases.*

SPECIALIZED TRAINING AND PREPARATION

Beyond the training and qualifications necessary for licensure, participation in child custody cases necessitates that the mental health practitioner obtain specialized training. As with so many areas of mental health practice, there is no single authoritative source for determining necessary training and preparation.

When faced with a question about competence and standard of care, the mental health practitioner should look for answers in laws and professional ethics and standards. Psychologists are told:

A psychologist contemplating performing child custody evaluations is aware that special competencies and knowledge are required for the undertaking of such evaluations. Competence in performing psychological assessments of children, adults, and families is necessary but not sufficient. Education, training, experience, and/or supervision in the areas of child and family development, child and family psychopathology, and the impact of divorce on children help to prepare the psychologist to participate competently in child custody evaluations. The psychologist also strives to become familiar with the applicable legal standards and procedures, including laws governing divorce and custody adjudications in his or her state of jurisdiction. (American Psychological Association, 1994, p. 678)

The latter should include laws on child abuse, neglect, and family violence. These guidelines go on to urge the psychologist to remain current, such as through continuing professional development, and avoid or seek consultation for cases that may be beyond assured expertise. Similarly, forensic psychologists are reminded that they should: "Provide services only in areas of psychology in which they have specialized knowledge, skill, experience, and education," and "are responsible for a fundamental and reasonable level of knowledge and understanding of the legal and professional standards that govern their participation as experts in legal proceedings" (Committee on Ethical Guidelines for Forensic Psychologists, 1991, p. 658).

Regarding statutes and rules, few jurisdictions have, to date, specified the minimal specialized training for involvement in child custody cases. In keeping with its reputation for micromanagement of psychological practices, the Florida Board of Psychology has promulgated the following rule:

> To perform psychological evaluation of minors for the purpose of making a forensic recommendation regarding custody or visitation, a psychologist must have training in child development and child psychopathology. In addition, the psychologist must have training in family dynamics, and in legal issues and guidelines regarding child custody. (Florida Administrative Code, Chapter 64B19-18.007[2])

Gindes (1995) suggests ways to obtain specialized training and preparation (e.g., peer forums). Too many mental health practitioners are prone to erroneously think that attending a seminar or reading a few books will provide adequate preparation for child custody services; equally faulty is the notion that participation as a witness in a child custody case, in and of itself, verifies competence.

➜ *Guideline: For purposes of both quality care and defending against an ethical, regulatory, or legal complaint, the mental health practitioner should obtain formal training (as opposed to, say, self education) in the substantive psychological, social, and legal issues that underlie child custody matters.*

Although other mental health disciplines may not specify required training and preparation, this absence does not create an exemption from liability. The mental health practitioner, regardless of professional discipline, would be wise to draw from the relevant information provided, such as for psychologists, and pursue specialized training accordingly.

THE CHILD CUSTODY EVALUATION

There are three components to child custody evaluations: "(1) comprehensive observations and interviewing of the parents and children and gathering of interview and archival information from third-party sources, (2) the administration of traditional psychological tests, and (3) the administration of specialized tests" (Melton et al., 1997, p. 501). As will be discussed, mental health practitioners (particularly psychologists) tend to rely heavily upon psychological tests, even some which have little or no reliability and validity vis-à-vis child custody determination (and test data certainly do not carry guidelines for a visitation schedule per se).

As relevant to psychological testing, it is noteworthy that the National Conference of Commissioners on Uniform State Laws, an august group of legal scholars who formulate the uniform laws for possible adoption by state legislatures, early on issued a less than positive statement about the use of psychological assessment in marriage and divorce law:

> Psychological research that can be considered both relevant and useful to the problems of custody adjudication is minimal. . . . Similarly, judgments based upon psychological tests for either the parents or the child are not likely to be well founded, since there is little evidence that such test results have any implications in terms of the person's actual behavior. The same is true of individual personality assessments made by psychologists and psychiatrists. (Ellsworth & Levy, 1969, p. 198)

As will be explained, psychological testing should not be abandoned, but it should be balanced appropriately with other types of information or data.

Some courts seem in awe of psychological tests, while others express skepticism. I heard one judge pronounce, "There will never be a day when I let a bunch of inkblots determine the custody of a child."

What do courts prefer? It seems that greatest weight is given to observational information from a credible source, such as a mental health practitioner who has interviewed persons and conducted a site visit to the location where the child might be living or visiting. I believe that both interviews with extended family (and others) and site visits are too often neglected by mental health practitioners (to their credit, social workers tend to rely the most on these two information-gathering methods).

➜ *Guideline: The mental health practitioner should accept that comprehensive observations, interviewing, and site visits, buttressed by, say, psychological testing, is the approach of choice for a child custody evaluation.*

Deciding whether or not to use psychological tests remains for professional discretion. The decision should be based on the unique attributes of the case at hand. Stated differently, it is feasible that some testimony about a child custody case would not require psychological test data. Further, the mental health practitioner planning to use psychological tests should determine whether traditional or specialized instruments are needed, and it is highly improbable that the same psychological tests should not be used in all child custody cases. The only caveat would be, of course, that the psychological tests used should fulfill the applicable test construction and ethical standards.

➜ *Guideline: The mental health practitioner should structure and tailor the evaluation to the unique characteristics of the case at hand, being sure that the data-collection methods are appropriate for the persons and issues (e.g., avoid using the same psychological test battery for all persons), and that they will yield reliable and valid information; any uncertainty about reliability and validity of information or data should be noted in the evaluation report and testimony.*

THE ROLE OF PROFESSIONAL DISCIPLINE IN THE EVALUATION

A threshold issue for decisions about child custody evaluation involves the professional discipline of the mental health practitioner. In keeping with the mandate that professional services should always be provided with competence, it is evident that certain

evaluation procedures or methods could be consonant or disso-
nant with role, functions, and competencies within the training for
a given mental health professional discipline. Stated differently, the
child custody evaluation conducted by, say, a clinical social worker
might (and logically would) be different from that conducted by
a mental health counselor, a marriage and family therapist, a psychologist, a psychiatrist, or a psychiatric nurse. Even more specifically, say among psychologists, the evaluations might differ
depending upon whether the evaluator was a clinical psychologist,
counseling psychologist, or school psychologist. In any event, both
the role(s) and functions endorsed for the particular mental health
discipline and the competencies of the given mental health practitioner must be accommodated.

→ *Guideline: In selecting methods for a child custody evaluation,
the mental health practitioner should recognize that there is no
single prescribed approach or set or information-gathering
methods; rather, the child custody evaluation must, among other
things, be based on the role(s) and functions deemed by public
policy and law to be appropriate for the professional discipline
and competencies of the particular mental health practitioner—
and the child custody evaluation reporting and testimony should
be tailored accordingly.*

A second threshold issue involves the reasons for the referral to
the mental health practitioner. As an example, assume that the referral is made by court order. If the referral is for a "home study,"
that is, a careful examination of the living conditions (including
psychosocial interactions), the child custody evaluation could be
potentially conducted by a competent mental health practitioner in
any of the professional disciplines. If the referral is, however, for a
"psychological evaluation" intended to provide an objective data-
based profile of the children, parents, and family members, this
type of evaluation would likely call for the service of a practitioner
in psychology. Of course, the referral and the best interests of the
child(ren) could result in all sorts of possible exceptional considerations for making choices relevant to the professional discipline or
between available practitioners (e.g., if a child has complex learning disabilities, a school psychologist might be more appropriate
than a clinical psychologist).

→ *Guideline: When defining the role and functions and considering professional discipline and competency, the substance of the referral must be carefully considered.*

To summarize, there is no one framework, format, or methodology for conducting child custody evaluations. For one suggested comprehensive approach, see Bricklin (1998), which includes a number of practical guidelines.

PSYCHOLOGICAL ASSESSMENT

Since psychological assessment figures prominently in child custody evaluations, it merits special emphasis. As stated in the preceding section, other types of mental health information can be of equal (and perhaps even greater) importance; and there is no one mental health professional discipline that has unimpeachable superiority for child custody evaluations and testimony.

In a replication of an earlier study by Keilin and Bloom (1986), M. J. Ackerman and M. C. Ackerman (1996) surveyed 800 psychologists, with 201 responding. As behavioral science, this 25% response rate tempers the ability to generalize the findings (note that these findings are also reported in M. J. Ackerman and M. C. Ackerman, 1997).

M. J. Ackerman and M. C. Ackerman (1996) found that the average evaluation process required 21.1 hours. The evaluation procedures (and the mean hours spent) were: observations (2.6); reviewing materials (2.6); collateral contacts (1.6); psychological testing (5.2); report writing (5.3); interviewing parents (4.7); interviewing children (2.7); interviewing significant others (1.6); consulting with attorneys (1.2); and testifying in court (2.2).

When it came to behavioral observations, the following reflect the percentages of practitioners carrying out these activities: observe each parent with each child alone (31.6%); observe each parent with all children together (59.2%); observe both parents with each child alone (4.4%); and observe both parents with all children together (4.8%). When doing a behavioral observation, 40.4% preferred using a structured task, while 59.6% did not.

When it came to psychological testing, 8.0% did not test children, 2.0% did not test adults, and 1.5% did not test either children or adults. Keeping in mind that the respondents were psychologists only, it is obvious that the child custody evaluations of this sample tend to embrace psychological testing. My personal experience with child custody cases supports that practitioners from each of the mental health disciplines can, and often do, make meaningful contributions to child custody evaluations and testimony.

What psychological tests are used for child custody evaluations? Rather than get into an exhaustive list of the tests that were identified in this study, the "Top Ten" for children/youth (derived from the percent of respondents who cited using the test, and the mean percent of the time that it was used) rank-ordered by usage were: intelligence tests, for example, Wechsler third edition, Stanford-Binet, Kaufman, and McCarthy (58.2% & 44.7%); children's and/or thematic apperception tests (36.8% & 52.8%); Bricklin perceptual scales (34.8% & 65.6%); sentence completion (29.4% & 76.3%); achievement test (27.9% & 56.0%); Rorschach inkblots (27.4% & 47.9%); miscellaneous projective drawings (24.4% & 72.1%); Minnesota Mulitphasic Personality Inventory-Adolescent (19.9% & 48.9%); house-tree-person (19.4% & 75.5%); and kinetic family drawing (18.4% & 86.9%).

For the evaluation of adults, the results were somewhat (but not dramatically) different. The "Top Ten" for adults (derived, respectively, from the percent of respondents who cited using the test, and the mean percent of the time that it was used) rank-ordered by usage were: Minnesota Multiphasic Personality Inventory (MMPI; both editions) (91.5% & 90.9%); Rorschach inkblots (47.8% & 63.6%); Wechsler Revised (42.8% & 49.3%); Millon Clinical Multiaxial Inventory (34.3% & 72.8%); thematic apperception test (29.4% & 56.2%); sentence completion (22.4% & 87.5%); Ackerman-Schoendorf Scales for Parent Evaluation of Custody (11.4% & 89.3%); Parent/Child Relationship Inventory (10.9% & 72.5%); Wide Range Achievement Test revised and third edition (10.4% & 78.3%); and projective drawings (9.0% & 74.9%).

In keeping with the purpose of a replication, M. J. Ackerman and M. C. Ackerman (1996) looked back at the Keilin and Bloom (1986) survey, and note that for children:

> The use of the Bender-Gestalt is down considerably compared to its usage ten years ago. In contrast, the usage of sentence completion tasks has increased significantly. Furthermore, drawing tasks, in general, including projective

drawings, the House-Tree-Person, and Kinetic-Family Drawing are used considerably more now than ten years ago. Although the Robert's [sic] Apperception Test has been in use for many years, it has not increased in usage over the past ten years. Although the Rorschach is lower on the list of preferred tests, the percentage of time that it is used has not changed noticeably either. (pp. 570 & 573)

Regarding the testing of adults, the conclusion is simple: "Four of the top five tests used in 1996 are the same as those used in 1986" (p. 577). Noting that the survey did not distinguish between the original and second versions of the MMPI, they add: "The MMPI has remained the most frequently used test, and in fact, is used by 20 percent more respondents now than it was ten years ago" (p. 573).

There are certain psychological tests that purport to evaluate child custody potentials (e.g., Ackerman-Schoendorf Scales for Parent Evaluation of Custody, M. J. Ackerman and Schoendorf, 1992; and the Bricklin Perceptual Scales, Bricklin, 1984). If these instruments had adequate psychometric properties, they would obviously be a boon to child custody evaluations and testimony. The survey of psychologists by M. J. Ackerman and M. C. Ackerman (1996) did not reveal great reliance on these specialized tests, and they note that, referencing the Keilin and Bloom (1986) survey, that the usage has "not changed substantially from 1986 to 1996" (p. 574). To date, however, professional criticism abounds, which is summarized by Melton et al. (1997): "Although some of these measures may facilitate gathering useful responses regarding parents' attitudes, knowledge, or values with respect to raising their children, the lack of adequate reliability and validity studies counsels against use of the formal indices they yield" (p. 504).

As mentioned before, the methods used for the child custody evaluation should be determined idiosyncratically for the particular case: "The scope of the custody-related evaluation is determined by the nature of the question or issue raised by the referring person or the court, or is inherent in the situations" (American Psychological Association, 1994, p. 678).

To accommodate the cognitive social-learning approach, the mental health practitioner should consider self reports and other methods that will reveal information of cognitions, behaviors, and reinforcement contingencies. As will be discussed in the next section, the family systems approach will also open up the possibility of special evaluation methods.

→ *Guideline: The mental health practitioner should not unquestionably base the child custody evaluation on the psychological tests that are reportedly used by most other professionals; notwithstanding current usage, there is reason to doubt the general appropriateness or adaptability of certain psychological tests for child custody purposes, and certainly reason to doubt that any particular test is appropriate for all persons in every child custody case.*

EVALUATING THE FAMILY SYSTEM

In keeping with integrating the cognitive social-learning and family systems approaches: "The primary consideration in a child custody evaluation is to assess the individual and family factors that affect the best psychological interests of the child" (American Psychological Association, 1994, p. 677). This statement makes it clear that factors relevant to family relationships should be assessed, which means that potentially the evaluation should include persons other than the child and parents.

Ideally (perhaps minimally), the mental health practitioner conducting a child custody evaluation should have extensive access to both parents. According to the "Guidelines for Child Custody Evaluations in Divorce Proceedings" (American Psychological Association, 1994), "Comprehensive child custody evaluations generally require an evaluation of all parents or guardians and children" (p. 678), and the focus should be on the parents' capacity to fulfill the child's psychological needs. Specifically, this calls for: "(a) an assessment of the adults' capacities for parenting, including whatever knowledge, attributes, skills, and abilities, or lack thereof, are present; (b) an assessment of the psychological functioning and developmental needs of each child and of the wishes of each child where appropriate; and (c) an assessment of the functional ability of each parent to meet these needs, including an evaluation of the interaction between each adult and child" (p. 678). In addition, the guidelines suggest: "Psychopathology may be relevant to such an assessment, insofar as it has impact on the child or the ability to parent, but it is not the primary focus" (p. 678).

If there is a lack of parental cooperation, the child custody evaluation will be compromised. Each parent may seek to be assessed individually by a mental health practitioner of his or her choosing. When this occurs, there are two possible problems. First, there will not be a single mental health practitioner who has an in-depth understanding of each and every person, and a comprehensive integration of the information and data may not be possible. Second, introducing more than one mental health practitioner creates the risk that the evaluation may become a "battle of the experts," where each mental health practitioner is tempted to one-up and discredit any testimony offered by other mental health practitioners that does not support fully his or her interpretation, opinions, and recommendations. The divergent views produced by a "battle of the experts" may appear to enhance the determinations made by the court, but it may also result in long-lasting detrimental effects for the child, the parents, and postdivorce family relations. Also, the mental health testimony from multiple practitioners will require greater financial expenditures, something that few parents going though child custody legal proceedings can afford.

By rule, the Florida Board of Psychology makes it clear that parents should be involved in the child custody evaluation:

> When an evaluation is for the purpose of making a recommendation to a court regarding custody, residence or visitation of a minor, the psychologist must, at least, communicate with the parties seeking custody of the minor or their legal representatives, and with the mental health professionals and the primary medical physician, if any, who are treating the minor, unless excused from doing so by court order. If a party fails to participate in the evaluation process, the psychologist shall so advise the court. (Florida Administrative Code, Chapter 64B19-18.007[1])

As the rule states, the parent who does not cooperate with the child custody evaluation will be subject to the judge's review.

The child custody evaluation should not, however, stop with information collected from the child and the parents; it should encompass information from significant others, such as siblings and extended family members:

> Nor should the evaluation stop with interviews of the im-
> mediate family. Contact with extended family, teachers,
> social services agencies, and even baby-sitters can illumi-
> nate potential sources of support (or the lack thereof) under
> various custody arrangements (e.g., switching between pa-
> rental homes). Sources outside the nuclear family may also
> give important, relatively objective glimpses of the chil-
> dren's responses to arrangements developed during separa-
> tions and under temporary custody orders. In that regard,
> the existing and previous custody arrangements can be
> conceptualized as natural experiments of a sort. The clini-
> cian should be sure to elicit information as to the parties'
> attitudes and behavioral response to those arrangements.
> (Melton et al., 1997, p. 501)

When evaluating other than the child and parents, the mental health
practitioner should verify the quality of the information obtained:
"If information is gathered from third parties that is significant and
may be used as a basis for conclusions, psychologists corroborate it
by at least one other source wherever possible and appropriate and
document this in the report" (American Psychological Association,
1994, p. 679).

When conducting an evaluation of the family system, the mental health practitioner will likely use specialized methods, such as a
structured family systems interview (which is developed from the
tenets of the family systems approach) (Worden, 1999) and a geno-
gram (which typically encompasses three generations) (Brock &
Barnard, 1999). As with the evaluation of an individual, the evaluation of a family system should be determined idiosyncratically,
that is, on a case-by-case basis.

➔ *Guideline: The child custody evaluation should go beyond the*
  child, definitely to the parents, and ideally to significant others
  in the child's present and future family and social systems; and
  the evaluation methods should be selected idiosyncratically.

THE SIX HARBINGERS OF DOOM

When considering role and functions, it is important to be on
guard against conditions that diminish the quality of the services
and lead to ethical, regulatory, or legal complaint against a mental

health practitioner. There are six problem areas that merit special consideration, each of which can be avoided or dealt with effectively through determining the role and functions that are or are not acceptable to the mental health practitioner. These problems evolve when the mental health practitioner succumbs to nonprofessional conduct; and although each has been discussed earlier in this book, deserves another mention for summary purposes.

First, the mental health practitioner who becomes involved in multiple roles is inviting a complaint. This problem has already been discussed so much that it need not be elaborated upon further at this time. Suffice it to repeat that the mental health practitioner should enter the child custody case with a clear and singular role.

Second, complainants often allege that the mental health practitioner made faulty interpretations, that is, overinterpreted or misjudged the information or data. The fault may be revealed by another mental health practitioner testifying in the same case. Of course this matter typically does not arise unless faulty interpretations are to the disadvantage of the complainant.

Third, testifying about a parent, a situation, or anything without firsthand knowledge of the circumstances certainly reduces the quality of the service, and is a surefire way for the mental health practitioner to incur a complaint. Even though there is an exception to hearsay evidence that would potentially allow a mental health practitioner to give an opinion based on diagnostic and treatment information that others in the professional discipline would rely upon (which might include secondhand accounts), child custody cases require that the mental health practitioner have direct and substantive contact with anyone about whom there will be evaluative or diagnostic opinion testimony. Since it is common for attorneys to push a mental health practitioner to opine about things well beyond firsthand knowledge and to respond to hypotheticals, the mental health practitioner can inadvertently be led across the line into malpractice by offering improper professional interpretations, opinions, and recommendations.

Fourth, performing treatment, evaluations, and other services for child custody cases requires special and advanced skills.

At one level, performance of a custody evaluation requires the same basic training and experience for the conduct of *any* clinical assessment. That is, one must be skilled in the administration and interpretation of measures and techniques to be used and well versed in psychometric issues relating to use of measurement instruments. In addition, one must have completed adequate training and developed a suitable level of skill in evaluating those populations (e.g., children, adults, mentally retarded persons) who might be the subject of the evaluation. Clearly, a clinician whose training and experience have been exclusively adult focused should not venture to conduct a clinical assessment of a child or to offer any statements about what conditions appear to promote or impede a child's optimum functioning. (Weithorn, 1987, p. 190)

Thus, a major source for diminished quality care and for ethical, regulatory, and legal complaints results when the mental health practitioner blindly wanders into child custody cases without adequate specialized or advanced training.

Fifth, any form of legal advocacy is likely to be perceived as inappropriate by at least one of the parents, namely because it appears to reduce the mental health practitioner's objectivity and impartial stance. The mental health practitioner should not "act as an advocating attorney, who strives to present his or her client's best possible case" (American Psychological Association, 1994, p. 678). If others in the case cannot accept that professional objectivity and impartiality are essential to the role and functions in child custody evaluations, the mental health practitioner "should consider withdrawing from the case" (p. 678). Stated bluntly, the mental health practitioner must allow no bias or discrimination, regardless of reason, to contaminate objectivity and impartiality. This would include stereotypes and preordained (unscientific) notions: "The psychologist recognizes and strives to overcome any such biases or withdraws from the evaluation" (p. 678).

Sixth and finally, the mental health practitioner should "not act as a judge, who makes the ultimate decision applying the law to all relevant evidence" (p. 678). Here again, proper role and functions require that the mental health practitioner leave the ultimate legal decisions to the trier of fact.

Chapter 7

MANAGING CHILD CUSTODY CASES

As compared to clinical (nonforensic) cases, providing mental health services to persons involved in child custody cases requires considerably more tactful management. The adversarial nature of the child custody legal proceedings, coupled with the unfortunate human foibles that are exposed in legal situations, carry the potential for negative effects for the clients and the mental health practitioner. The preceding chapter closed with discussion of six major problems that may occur in child custody cases. This chapter will discuss other pitfalls, and provide guidelines to obtain effective case management.

EFFECTIVE CASE MANAGEMENT

Provision of any kind of mental health service requires calculated case management. Decisions about communications, interactions, and services derive from both mental health and legal issues. In general, effective case management consists of seven components:

1. There should be a clear and acceptable definition for the service to be provided and for what and how services shall occur. Among other things, this definition should include the role and functions (e.g., the nature of the practitioner-client relationship), goals and objectives, the assessment and

intervention methods, and the anticipated communication of confidential and privileged information.

2. Written informed consent and authorization to release information should be obtained from all adults to whom services are provided or from whom information is obtained (note that children should be informed fully, and the adult[s] with guardianship should provide the written consent and authorization).

3. The reciprocal exchange—the payment that will be made by the client in exchange for the mental health practitioner's services—must be specified and accepted by all concerned.

4. The professional services must occur according to an individually tailored plan; and these services must, of course, be consonant with the mutually agreed upon role and functions, and professional ethics and standards.

5. The effectiveness of the professional services must be monitored, and changes made in the plan accordingly (note that changes may necessitate additional informed consent and authorization to release information).

6. Detailed and meaningful records must be made and preserved, as will potentially benefit both the client and the practitioner.

7. Any special conditions should be set forth.

For each of the foregoing tenets of effective case management, it is wise—and required in some jurisdictions—to have the intentions, understandings, commitments, responsibilities, and duties for both the client and the mental health practitioner stated clearly in writing. This is in accord with professional ethics and standards; for example, psychologists are expected to provide "appropriate information beforehand about the nature of such services and appropriate information later about results and conclusions" (American Psychological Association, 1992, p. 1600).

➜ *Guideline: The mental health practitioner should construct and maintain an individually tailored case management system that maximizes the quality and propriety of the services (including appropriate role and functions) and minimizes the deleterious effects caused by the adversarial nature of child custody cases.*

TERMINATION AND WITHDRAWAL FROM THE CASE

Each tenet of effective case management will necessarily be subject to revision. If a request or reason for change in the role and functions of the mental health practitioner emerges that is unacceptable to either of the parties (or their attorneys) or to the mental health practitioner, the mental health practitioner may have to tactfully bow out of the case; that is, if disagreement about the role and functions cannot be resolved satisfactorily, termination of services by the mental health practitioner may be advisable. Said differently, neither of the parents nor the mental health practitioner should be expected to continue in a professional relationship under impositions or conditions that are not fully acceptable or proper.

The mental health practitioner must only provide services that: are in the best interests of the client; honor the practitioner's rights; and are in accord with the public policies, laws, and professional ethics and standards. Therefore, a request (or demand) from a client (or the client's attorney) that could subvert the quality or propriety of any essential aspect of the professional relationship could trigger consideration of termination of the mental health practitioner's services. Depending on the circumstances, termination or withdrawal from the case might require the approval of the court (e.g., if the mental health practitioner were court-appointed to the case).

➔ *Guideline: When disagreements over the role and functions emerge and cannot be resolved, the mental health practitioner should consider withdrawing from a child custody case and give notice as required.*

WHO IS THE CLIENT?

At first blush in a child custody case, it would seem that the answer to the question "Who is the client?" would be simply that the child is the client. Certainly the best interests of the child test calls for clarification of this question.

A similar notion about client status connects to who sought or who is paying for the professional services of the mental health practitioner. This idea is, however, faulty, because a person with interests quite alien to the best interests of the child could be the one contacting the mental health practitioner or paying for the professional services. In this scenario, the practitioner would not elevate the contact or payment source's interests above the best interests of the child.

In clinical cases, it is relatively easy to identify the "client." Identification of the "client" is more difficult in forensic cases in general and child custody cases in specific. That is, the problems of identifying to whom the mental health practitioner is duty bound is compounded by public policy, laws, and professional ethics and standards. A preordained answer to the question "Who is the client?" is impossible, and any attempt otherwise may be misleading (Hill, 1998).

This is an era when third-party sources have entered into the professional relationship. Stated differently, the revered "therapeutic alliance," once reserved solely for the client and the mental health practitioner, has been augmented by third-party payment sources (e.g., health insurance companies, managed care organizations, etc.), government regulators (e.g., licensing board personnel), and—with child custody cases—attorneys, court workers, and judges. Each of these sources believes that the mental health practitioner has a legal duty to fulfill its expectations.

In identifying the "client" in a child custody case, Melton et al. (1997) state:

> First, it is the *child's* interests, not the parties' (i.e., the parents') interests that are theoretically paramount; accordingly, some of the usual reasons for protecting the interests of the parties do not so readily apply. That is, there may be substantial reason for the court to seek its own evidence as to the interests of a third party (i.e., the child). Second, as a practical matter, it is difficult to do a credible custody evaluation without access to both parents. Yet, under a pure adversarial approach, the clinician would have no basis for rendering an opinion about the parent not employing the clinician. Even if the clinician is asked to address only the effects that may occur if custody is granted to the employing party, he or she is hampered by not hearing the other parent's side of things, because the family history and family process are likely to be perceived differently by each party. Accordingly, as a general rule, we suggest that clinicians seek to enter custody disputes as an expert for the court or the guardian *ad litem*, although there may be some

rare circumstances in which it is sufficient to have access to only one parent. (p. 500; citations omitted)

From the quotation, it is clear that there is no single source to whom the mental health practitioner owes allegiance. Consequently, the responsibilities and duties (as well as the role and functions) of the mental health practitioner should be determined cautiously and with the assistance of the court.

Certainly being named by the court to be an evaluator, mediator, guardian *ad litem*, or expert is the preferable entry for the mental health practitioner, but that may not be possible. As Melton et al. state in the last sentence of the preceding quotation, it may be only one parent who brings the mental health practitioner into the child custody case; if so, this will impose a restriction on the role and functions.

Returning to the responsibilities and duties associated with the designated client, consideration should also be given to the idea that contemporary mental health practice supports promotion of healthy and constructive conditions in the child's present and future family system. Therefore, an element of the definition of client status is the family system.

To answer specifically the topic question, "Who is the client?," there is no one client, not even the child. The "client" is an amorphous aggregate of all of the persons involved in the child custody case (i.e., the child, the parents, other family members, the attorneys and the judge, and on and on), as well as the sources of the public policies, laws, and professional ethics and standards by which the mental health practitioner provides services.

Consider the possibility of confidentiality for collateral sources (which will be discussed in greater detail later in the next chapter), such as a grandparent who provides information for a child custody evaluation. If the grandparent would not have made the communications but for the mental health practitioner's professional role and functions in the child custody case, and the grandparent reasonably intended and interpreted the communications with the mental health practitioner to be "professional," it would seem that the grandparent could be conceptualized as being a "client." To exemplify the legal duty that would seemingly arise in that scenario, if the interaction with the grandparent included the mental health practitioner's rendering an opinion or a recommendation upon which the grandparent relied to his or her detriment (e.g., the grandparent incurred injury or damages based on what was said by the mental health practitioner), it would seem that the grandparent would have a possible cause of action for a lawsuit against the mental health practitioner.

Today, it is faulty to attempt to accord special rights or protection to a single person, regardless of the conditions surrounding the mental health practitioner's entry into the child custody case. The modern view seems to be that communication, not payment, determines the answer to "Who is the client?"

➡ *Guideline: The mental health practitioner should award "client" status (and the attendant rights and protections) to anyone with whom the mental health practitioner communicates in the process of providing professional services; and secondary sources (such as the interests of society and the legal system) must also be considered.*

➡ *Guideline: Rather than sense a primary alliance or advocacy for any one person or "client" in the child custody case, the mental health practitioner should support high quality services for all persons and sources that have a stake in the legal proceedings.*

CONTRACTUAL AGREEMENTS

Although there are differences between jurisdictions, laws in general and professional ethics and standards pertaining to all of the mental health disciplines favor providing professional services according to agreed upon terms and conditions. In child custody cases, it is especially important to specify the fee arrangement, how legal discovery (e.g., a subpoena) will be handled, and the communication of confidential information. Ideally, this agreement would be in a written contract, thereby documenting the rights and duties aligned with both the client(s) and the mental health practitioner.

FINANCIAL AGREEMENTS

Financial agreements should be made from the outset of services. Here again, there is support from law and professional ethics and standards. For example, "As early as feasible in a professional or scientific relationship, the psychologist and the patient, client, or other appropriate recipient of psychological services reach an agreement specifying the compensation and the billing arrangements" (American Psychological Association, 1992, p. 1602).

In their survey of psychologists, M. J. Ackerman and M. C. Ackerman (1996) addressed the issue of fees. Keep in mind that they found that the average child custody evaluation required 21.1 hours:

> The average hourly fee reported for psychological testing was $120.63, while the average hourly fee for testifying was $154.77; 41.0 percent of the respondents had the same hourly fee for testing as they did for testifying. The range of fees for testing was $45 to $250, while the range for testifying was $40 to $500. The average fees for custody evaluations ranged from $650 to $15,000 with the average cost being $2,645.96. The average fee for a custody evaluation has almost tripled in the past ten years. (p. 575)

M. J. Ackerman and M. C. Ackerman found that 50.5% of the respondents preferred a full retainer before providing psychological testing, while only 5.1% required no retainer. Partial retainers were required by the remainder.

Getting paid after having provided psychological services in a custody case is a common problem. M. J. Ackerman and M. C. Ackerman found that full payment in advance of testifying was required by 83%, while 6.3% required partial payment in advance and 10.3% had no requirement.

COLLECTING PROFESSIONAL FEES

Child custody cases present the mental health practitioner with numerous fee-related problems. Since a divorce is so costly, both financially and psychologically, the impending decline in income often triggers an effort by the parties to avoid paying experts, or at least to pay as little or as slowly as possible.

In service to advocacy of their clients, some attorneys try to take advantage of a mental health practitioner. For example, an attorney may want to pay the mental health practitioner for only the actual time spent on the stand testifying, notwithstanding the fact that the same attorney may require the mental health practitioner to, say, block out the entire day, spend time traveling to the courthouse, and wait around throughout the trial while other testimony is taken.

A major problem arises when the attorney who wants to oppose the mental health practitioner's testimony uses legal process (e.g., a subpoena) to require a deposition, and attempts to characterize the mental health practitioner as a "fact" witness, while trying to obtain interpretations, opinions, and recommendations that clearly reach to the expertise of the mental health practitioner. The fee for "fact" testimony is usually nominal, as opposed to the regular professional fee to which the expert witness would be entitled.

The possibility of lost income or abuse of professional expertise should be opposed mightily. Elsewhere, I have provided details about these matters (Woody, 1997, 2000). For this discussion, it is sufficient to say that, before providing any services, the mental health practitioner should:

- Seek a clear fee arrangement with the attorneys and clients (on both sides of the case), and reduce it to a written contract.
- Understand any legal implications for fees that may be unique to the jurisdiction (e.g., some states have statutes that allow the court to impose a fixed or reasonable fee on the expert, or that require a treating therapist to provide both fact and expert testimony for only the fact-witness compensation).
- Be prepared to assertively pursue a remedy for improper or stonewalling efforts by either or both of the attorneys.

For example, if an attorney has refused to agree to pay the mental health practitioner for expert testimony, the mental health practitioner should, upon being sworn in on the stand to testify, politely interrupt the proceedings and inform the judge that there is a conflict, explain the fee schedule, and request that the judge issue a ruling on fees.

When dealing with a fee dispute—and at all other times as well—it is important for the mental health practitioner to convey great respect and support for the judicial system and a stance of good citizenship. At the same time, the mental health practitioner can underscore that he or she is appearing to testify relevant to a client and that the testimony will call for reliance on professional education and training that was costly for the mental health practitioner to obtain.

If all else fails, there is always the possibility of eventually taking legal action to collect unpaid fees. Often the amount of money, however, is small enough that pursuing a legal remedy is not financially feasible. For example, an unpaid bill for forensic services of, say, even a few thousand dollars, might require so much time that an attorney would be prone to decline to take the case on a contingency fee, and an hourly fee would have to be paid to the attorney. In making the expenditure to the attorney, the mental health practitioner would be faced with the fact that there is no guaranteed positive judgment or collection; thus, a legal action might be possible but not logical. Also, it is well established that when a mental health practitioner makes an effort to collect a debt from a client, even though justifiable, the likelihood increases that the client will file an ethical, regulatory, or legal complaint (Wright, 1981).

When faced with a mental health practitioner's effort to collect fees, some attorneys are, with all due respect, impolite and abrasive. If there is seemingly improper conduct or communications by an attorney, the mental health practitioner can consider filing a complaint with the ethics committee of the state bar association. When this possibility is posed in a polite, matter-of-fact manner, some attorneys wisely move toward a constructive resolution of the fee dispute.

➤ *Guideline: When providing professional services in a child custody case, the mental health practitioner should have a written contract that specifies any and all terms that will govern the relationship and services, including (but not limited to) fees and billing.*

➤ *Guideline: A retainer for the estimated minimum number of hours of service for the child custody case should be required.*

➤ *Guideline: Although it is possible to have fees differ according to the particular service provided, it is best to have a uniform fee, that is charged on a portal-to-portal basis.*

Client management in child custody cases is complex, problematic, and potentially treacherous. The prudent mental health practitioner will: become knowledgeable about the legal and professional issues encountered in child custody cases; develop effective methods for assuring quality care and safeguarding against ethical, regulatory, and legal complaints; and have an attorney readily available for consultation as needed. Although true for any type of mental health services, the foregoing need to have a legal ally is much more pronounced in forensic services in general and child custody cases in particular.

Chapter 8

PROTECTING MENTAL HEALTH INFORMATION

Professional ethics and standards give the utmost of importance to safeguarding the rights of clients. In child custody cases, perhaps the foremost problem is maintaining confidentiality and privileged communication, which connects into what is contained in mental health records, how the mental health practitioner handles legal discovery efforts, and the substance of courtroom testimony. Alleged failure to safeguard or handle confidential information is the basis for a substantial portion of the ethical, regulatory, and legal complaints filed against mental health practitioners. Further, protecting confidentiality and privileged communication constitutes a critical aspect of case management.

CONFIDENTIALITY AND PRIVILEGED COMMUNICATION

In child custody cases, protecting confidentiality and privileged communication is complex and risky. The intervention modality (e.g., seeing multiple family members) and the adversarial framework surrounding the mental health practitioner's involvement in a child custody case (e.g., which is subject to legal discovery strategies, such as a subpoena or court order for clinical records) create profound jeopardy for safeguarding confidential information.

Seeing a couple together presents certain legal and logical problems. Legal protection is often restricted to information that is truly secret, that is, not made available voluntarily to any other person.

Thus, when the mental health practitioner sees both the husband and wife, session notes are apt to reflect communications between the persons, as well as individually and collectively to and from the therapist. Since one spouse heard what the other spouse said or was told, a question is raised about the appropriateness of asserting confidentiality if a legal dispute should arise between the two later on.

By common law and sometimes by statute, the fact that both the husband and wife were present at the time of the communications eliminates a legally based claim to privileged communication between the spouses. The matter should, however, be determined by legal process, not by the mental health practitioner. That is, if one partner wants the mental health practitioner to not disclose what was said in the presence of the other partner, the mental health practitioner would be advised to seek an order from the court about whether the information deserves legal protection or not.

Going a step further than the preceding principle, legal discovery procedures, such as a subpoena or court order, can foster a dilemma for the mental health practitioner. For example, if the husband issues a subpoena for the wife's mental health records, but the wife tells her therapist that she does not want her records released, the therapist is left out on a limb. Given the subpoena, the wife could file a motion for a protective order, which—if granted by the court—would block the release of her records. If, however, the wife does not file such a motion and obtain a court order, yet tells the therapist to not release the record, the therapist could be subject to a motion for contempt of court. (Rather than getting into how to deal with legal discovery procedures, refer to American Psychological Association [1996b] and Woody [1997, 2000], which provide details on these matters.)

Especially noteworthy is the ethical recognition given to safeguarding individual rights when family interventions are provided. When dealing with a waiver of confidentiality, the ethics code for the American Association for Marriage and Family Therapy (AAMFT; 1998) states: "In circumstances where more than one person in a family receives therapy, each such family member who is legally competent to execute a waiver must agree to the waiver" (Section 2.1). Although the ethics codes for other mental health associations are not as specific, the foregoing AAMFT ethic is consonant with risk management for the practitioner, regardless of professional discipline. Even though common law may not support confidentiality for what is said between, say, parents, it is prudent to always obtain an express waiver from every person involved in the verbal exchange or to request a judicial order on the matter. More is said about this problem elsewhere, and particularly in Woody (2000).

Authorization to release confidential information requires informed consent. For child custody matters, the mental health practitioner should inform adult participants (and children as much as possible) from the outset about the evaluation and how the data may be used and specifically ensuring that "each adult participant is aware of (a) the purpose, nature, and method of the evaluation; (b) who has requested the psychologist's services; and (c) who will be paying the fees" (American Psychological Association, 1994, p. 679). Regardless of legal procedure, the mental health practitioner should obtain "a waiver of confidentiality from all adult participants or from their authorized legal representatives" (p. 679). Note "authorized legal representatives" seems to point toward an attorney's being able to waive privileged communication on behalf of his or her client. This may or may not be supported in a particular jurisdiction, and should be verified accordingly.

It is feasible that these third parties will be vested with a right to privileged communication, and their express authorization to release the information that they provided should be obtained (Woody, 2000). The criteria for justifying confidentiality includes what the communicator reasonably believed would be kept confidential.

Recall the example in the preceding chapter of how a grandparent who provides information in a child custody case might be deemed a client. Simply because the grandparent is not a party to the action, does not mean that the grandparent waived any claim to confidentiality. Depending on the circumstances, the grandparent might have a reasonable basis for expecting a right to confidentiality.

Regardless of circumstances, informed consent to release information and data for purposes of child custody cases should be obtained from all sources of communication. It should be remembered that true informed consent cannot be obtained before the communication occurs. Thus, the limits of confidentiality should be explained and acknowledged by the source prior to the communication, but the waiver of objection to releasing communications should occur after the communication has been made. If the source should refuse to authorize release of the information, even after having been told at the outset that confidentiality was limited or nonexistent, the matter can and should be put to the court for a legal determination. The mental health practitioner cannot be a quasi-judge about the issue of confidentiality. (Greater detail on these issues is available in Woody [2000].)

➔ *Guideline: A written authorization to release information and data should be obtained from each person with whom the mental health practitioner has communicated during the child custody case, notwithstanding being court-ordered to provide the services in general.*

➔ *Guideline: If a court order documents that there is no confidentiality for information obtained from any source contacted in child custody evaluation or other services, the mental health practitioner should inform each person at the outset accordingly and seek a written acknowledgment from the person that he or she understands; and after the communication has occurred, the mental health practitioner should seek a written acceptance of the lack of confidentiality and an authorization to release what was communicated.*

➔ *Guideline: In the event that a source of information rescinds (orally or in writing) his or her willingness to authorize the release of information or data obtained for purposes of a child custody case, the mental health practitioner should inform the court of the rescission and move the court for an order protecting or compelling the release of the information or data.*

LEGAL DISCOVERY AND CONFIDENTIALITY

Other aspects of confidentiality and privileged communication require the mental health practitioner to respond to legal discovery procedures. As mentioned, by common (case) law and often by statutory law, when a person becomes a party to a legal action, there is potentially an exception to confidentiality or privileged communication created for that person's mental health (and other) information, whether it is in clinical records or in testimony by the mental health practitioner. Also, legal discovery procedures, such as use of a subpoena, allow for incursions into information that would potentially merit status as confidential or privileged communication.

Whether commanding production of mental health records or the appearance of the mental health practitioner for a deposition or in a courtroom, a subpoena should be viewed as a positive process:

> A subpoena is a court document that orders a person to appear in court for a hearing or trial or at another location to be questioned regarding a pending lawsuit. Persons receiving a subpoena must comply unless the subpoena is withdrawn or is overruled by a judge. The penalty for noncompliance could include incarceration in jail or a fine. (Remley, 1991, p. 7)

A subpoena specifies that the mental health practitioner is subject to legal process, and is not on a course of self-determined advocacy.

Professional ethics and standards may well go further than the laws of the jurisdiction. It seems that the contemporary professional view is that the mental health practitioner, regardless of discipline, should inform the client about the limits of confidentiality, but also, on occasion, step forward to attempt to protect the confidentiality on behalf of the client. In other words, there may be commands or demands made by legal sources, such as through a subpoena, that will require actions by the mental health practitioner to reconcile the law with professional ethics and standards (see American Psychological Association, 1996a, 1996b, and Woody, 2000).

When parents engage in a legal dispute over child custody or visitation, the mental health records of either parent are potentially discoverable for use in the legal proceedings. On the other hand, simply having a child custody case before the court does not mean that the mental health practitioner should assume automatic waiver of, or exception to, a client's right to confidentiality or privileged communication. A judge may, however, declare a waiver or exception via a court order.

While a subpoena may authoritatively require production of a client's mental health records or testimony, the mental health practitioner should always confirm that the client knows about the subpoena and determine the client's wishes about the mental health practitioner's response to it. Regardless of legal procedure, the mental health practitioner should obtain "a waiver of confidentiality from all adult participants or from their authorized legal representatives" (American Psychological Association, 1994, p. 679).

The mental health practitioner's best response will depend on the facts of the case and the laws of the jurisdiction, but may include:

- Explaining the situation to the attorney who issued the subpoena, and suggesting that he or she file a motion to compel (if this is the action of choice, the mental health practitioner should make it clear that the client's objection has left the mental health practitioner in the awkward situation of wanting to honor the legal system, but being expected by professional ethics and standards to support the client); or
- entering a motion requesting that the judge rule on the matter (if this is the action of choice, the mental health practitioner, again, should make it clear that the effort in no way reflects his or her personal preferences, only a commitment to meeting the professional ethics and standards that pertain to protecting a client's welfare).

Although both of these strategies have a sound professional rationale and are consonant with law in general, the onus to do the right thing is placed on the mental health practitioner, and a misstep could be problematic and costly. Avoiding the problems associated with challenging a subpoena can be accomplished, in part, by maintaining an impartial, nonadvocacy stance.

➜ *Guideline: The mental health practitioner should never ignore a subpoena.*

One mental health practitioner chose to "blow-off the subpoena," and was held in civil contempt of court and fined $500. A blemish of this nature could haunt one's professional reputation for years to come, and could also spawn ethical, regulatory, or legal complaints.

➜ *Guideline: To all concerned, the mental health practitioner should state unreserved support and respect for the judicial system and respond to the legal process in a meaningful and timely manner.*

The preceding guideline is intended to circumvent a disgruntled attorney's alleging misconduct by the mental health practitioner. By establishing a clear-cut commitment to, and cooperation with, the legal system, the mental health practitioner can dispel any notion that might be used to construct a motion for contempt of court.

It should be noted that certain attorneys assert that a subpoena is a court order. Perhaps some sort of rationale can be developed for that definition, but a subpoena can be challenged, as described previously. An order signed by a judge is, however, another matter. Of course a judge's order can potentially be appealed, but for all intents and purposes, an appeal would be an option for the client who is a party to the action. At the point when a judge signs an order, the mental health practitioner has likely fulfilled any responsibility or duty assigned by public policy, laws, or professional ethics and standards to safeguard and defend the rights of a client. Unless there are exceptional circumstances and contrary legal advice has been obtained, the mental health practitioner's only subsequent action should likely be to respond to the judge's order.

There might be, of course, a rare exception, in which a mental health practitioner might take exception to a judge's order, such as filing a motion for rehearing. This action should only be taken upon the advice of an attorney licensed in the jurisdiction.

I have had several occasions when the attorneys for the parties appeared before the court and stipulated that they both wanted the mental health practitioner to provide entire kits for certain psychological tests. The mental health practitioner was not notified and did not appear at the hearing on the matter, yet was subject to a judge's order that would have potentially constituted a governmental taking of personal property and an order to violate professional ethics and standards. This scenario creates exceptional circumstances. In each instance, a motion for a rehearing led to a reasonable resolution of the problem, namely: the attorneys were given an opportunity to view selected portions of the psychological test kits and receive an orientation from the mental health practitioner; and the mental health practitioner was able to retain the psychological tests kits and, as expected by professional ethics and standards, preserve the integrity of the testing materials.

There are many twists and turns in legal processes relevant to mental health information, such as how to respond to a subpoena for test data (American Psychological Association, 1996a) or for the records of a deceased person (Burke, 1995). These and many other possible issues make having legal counsel readily available to the mental health practitioner a necessity of modern-day practice, albeit an unwelcomed additional expense for doing business. In addition to the two preceding citations, further information about responding to a subpoena and other forms of legal discovery can be found in American Psychological Association (1996b), and Woody (1997, 2000).

→ *Guideline: The mental health practitioner should obtain legal counsel to be sure that the response to legal discovery procedures is appropriate for the case and the jurisdiction.*

MENTAL HEALTH RECORDS

Again, according to public policy, laws (with possible differences between jurisdictions), and professional ethics and standards, the mental health practitioner, regardless of discipline, must keep written records that accurately, meaningfully, and completely reflect the nature and quality of services that were provided to the client. The records serve two purposes, both of which are essential to successful practice.

First, the mental health records provide documentation of what services the client received and what was experienced (i.e., the effects) because of the service. The notion is that, in the event that the client seeks services from another mental health practitioner later on, the decision about follow-up services would be enriched by knowing what had and had not produced desirable effects in the earlier services.

Second, the mental health records provide the mental health practitioner with invaluable risk management. A contemporaneously made written record of what occurred in a professional relationship will likely receive great weight when counteracting ethical, regulatory, or legal complaints.

→ *Guideline: The mental health practitioner should keep written records that reflect accurately, meaningfully, and completely the nature and quality of services that were provided to the client, thereby providing benefits to both the client (e.g., for future services from another mental health practitioner) and the mental health practitioner (e.g., for defending against ethical, regulatory, or legal complaints).*

Mental health records should be prepared with an expectation that other sources will read them at some point in the future. Thus, the contents and language should be tailored, in part, for the client, attorneys, and other mental health practitioners. Furthermore, no one can predict who else will have access to the mental health records or for what reason.

➡ *Guideline: The mental health practitioner should prepare mental health records with the knowledge that they will be accessed by unknown sources and used for unpredictable reasons; and the mental health practitioner should, therefore, be prepared to defend each and every entry in the record for its accuracy, relevancy, and appropriateness for the professional services that were provided.*

In this day and age, mental health records should be highly detailed, objectively stated, and in writing. If the professional service is clinical in nature, it is wise to formulate and execute the professional services according to an individualized treatment plan (Woody, 1991). The American Psychological Association (1993) has offered useful guidelines for mental health record keeping.

➡ *Guideline: The mental health practitioner should prepare records that reveal a professionally calculated plan of service (including a monitoring for quality care).*

The mental health practitioner is not expected to screen or censure the information that is entered into the mental health records according to whether it might be viewed as a positive or negative for the client by some other source. Stated bluntly, the mental health practitioner is not supposed to second-guess the use of the information by legal sources—the task is to include all information that is clinically significant, notwithstanding the effects for the client in a legal proceeding.

In child custody cases, the mental health practitioner is expected to include all information in the mental health records that is potentially significant, relevant, and material for the reasons for which the client sought and received the professional services, and as is consonant with the role and functions assigned to the mental health practitioner. Good faith judgments by the mental health practitioner determine what information merits inclusion in the mental health records. These judgments must, of course, be consonant with the prevailing ethics and standards for the profession, as well as with the public policies and laws that pertain to professional practice. Although there can be exceptions, a rule of thumb is that information that would be considered significant by a reasonable and prudent mental health practitioner should be included in the mental health records. There is little, if any, leeway for personal idiosyncrasies about this matter.

➡️ *Guideline: The mental health practitioner should include all information in the mental health records that is potentially significant, relevant, and material for the reasons for which the client sought and received the professional services, that is, information that a reasonable and prudent mental health practitioner would include in the mental health records.*

➡️ *Guideline: The mental health practitioner should not attempt to expurgate the information according to whether it would be viewed as a positive or negative for the client by some other source, such as by the court in a child custody legal proceeding.*

Mental health records must be preserved in accord with laws and professional ethics and standards. For example, the length of time that mental health records must or should be retained will vary with the jurisdiction and the professional discipline. It is advisable to obtain legal counsel about the laws of the jurisdiction that govern mental health records, and retention in specific.

Retention of records also depends in part on the nature of the professional services provided and the needs of the particular client. Professional ethics and standards for the mental health practitioner's discipline should be studied and followed.

For risk management purposes, the longer the complete mental health records are retained, the more potential evidence there will be for defense against ethical, regulatory, or legal complaints at some future time. Given the epidemic of complaints against mental health practitioners, risk management supports keeping complete records as long as it is pragmatically possible, even if it is longer than the minimum prescribed by law and professional ethics and standards.

➡ *Guideline: The mental health practitioner should retain records in a manner and for a duration defined by the relevant legal jurisdiction and professional discipline, with consideration of the nature of the professional services provided and the needs of the particular client, as well as the risk management benefits for defending against ethical, regulatory, and legal complaints.*

INFORMED CONSENT

All mental health services should be prefaced by written informed consent by the client. Note that, even if not specified by law per se, a written document for informed consent or any other type of authorization provides a legal safety net for the benefit of both the client and the mental health practitioner.

The term "informed consent" has relevance to two major aspects of child custody cases: the services that will be provided; and the release of mental health information. Child custody legal proceedings introduce some special concerns and problems in both of these areas.

The person may be under duress to receive the mental health services. The duress jeopardizes true consent. For example, if a parent was ordered by the court to participate in a child custody evaluation, he or she may be literally forced to provide information involuntarily.

Although such a mandate for participation may be legally proper, the mental health practitioner is not relieved of upholding professional ethics and standards. This challenge will necessitate the mental health practitioner's making a special effort to ameliorate resistance on the part of the client, provide extensive education about the process to the client, and possibly assert to the court and other sources (on behalf of the client) that certain conditions should be applied to the provision of professional services.

➡ *Guideline: The mental health practitioner should take appropriate steps to assure that a client's participation in the professional services is with knowledge of the nature and purpose, and that information is given voluntarily.*

Before providing any services at all, it is common for a mental health practitioner to ask a new client to sign a written authorization for the information that will be garnered during a child custody evaluation that is to be released to, say, the attorneys, guardian *ad litem*, and judge. While it is appropriate and prudent to have a client acknowledge from the outset that he or she has been informed about the services and is participating willingly (if that is, in fact, the case), it is obvious that any authorization to release information that does not yet exist is not truly informed consent. Stated differently, a person cannot be informed about what information is going to be released to, say, the court when the information has not yet been produced. This means, of course, that informed consent must be confirmed over and over throughout the mental health services that are provided in the child custody legal proceedings.

➔ *Guideline: Knowing that informed consent is not a once-only determination, the mental health practitioner should repeatedly provide the client with information about the immediate service, and obtain written informed consent accordingly.*

Obtaining informed consent is not a simple matter. To clarify the elements of informed consent, consider the following standard from the ethics for psychologists: "The content of informed consent will vary depending on many circumstances; however, informed consent generally implies that the person (1) has the capacity to consent, (2) has been informed of significant information pertaining to the procedure, (3) has freely and without undue influence expressed consent, and (4) consent has been appropriately documented" (American Psychological Association, 1992, p. 1605). Relatedly, the child custody guidelines from the American Psychological Association (1994) support, from the start of services, informing adult participants (and children as much as possible) about the evaluation and how the data may be used—the psychologist is expected to ensure that "each adult participant is aware of (a) the purpose, nature, and method of the evaluation; (b) who has requested the psychologist's services; and (c) who will be paying the fees" (p. 679).

To document informed consent for psychological services, Bennett et al. (1990) recommend including:

1. date of discussion regarding consent
2. your name and the patient's name, preferably typed

3. a sentence affirming that the client understood what he or she was told
4. a statement of the client's right to withdraw consent
5. a description of the kind of treatment to be provided (this may be particularly relevant if experimental treatment is being offered)
6. a signature of the client or parent or guardian. (p. 49)

If the informed consent is for the release of confidential information (be it in records or testimony), the particular situation should be considered (e.g., the purpose for which the information will be used, who will have access to the information, and so on). A written authorization should generally include "evidence that the client knew the purpose served and the possible positive and negative consequences resulting from the release of the information; authorized the particular receiver of the information (e.g., by name or facility); was aware of what was contained in the records or information that would be released; and had mental competency and was voluntarily granting the waiver of confidentiality (e.g., there was neither mental duress nor undue influence from the therapist)" (Woody, 1997, p. 72). Also see Koocher (1998) for other ideas on the elements of consent forms.

Chapter 9

TESTIFYING IN CHILD CUSTODY CASES

The proverbial welcome mat has been placed out for mental health practitioners to cross the threshold into the courtroom. Being cloaked in the robes of respectability fashioned by the academy, mental health practitioners of every ilk may now make pronouncements about countless legal issues, including those in child custody cases.

Expert testimony by mental health practitioners is justified by their bringing scholarly, behavioral science, and experiential information to the court that will assist the trier of fact (the judge or a jury) make legal determinations. As mentioned several times before, their entry was not intended to create a substitute trier of fact. More will be said later about the purpose of expert testimony.

There have been allegations that expert opinions are elastic and can be shaped to support any opinion or prediction, which if true would lead to faulty child custody determinations (Okpaku, 1976). Along this line, testimony by mental health practitioners is often assailed: "The introduction of expert testimony in legal proceedings, particularly testimony regarding social and behavioral scientific evidence, has rarely been accomplished without controversy" (Goodman-Delahunty, 1997, p. 122).

The doubts about mental health testimony lead to aspersions; for example: "As seriously flawed as psychiatric and psychological testimony can be, such errors are not readily recognizable except by those who are well-acquainted with the relevant research literature" (Campbell, 1994, p. 68). This means that, consciously or unconsciously, mental health practitioners may convey misleading or false information to the trier of fact, thereby contradicting the reason the public policy and law welcomed their participation in the legal proceedings, and of concern in this book on child custody, jeopardizing the best interests of the child, the family, and society.

The crux of the matter is two-fold. First, there is question about the scientific quality of the mental health testimony. Second, there is question about the relevance of mental health research to child custody per se.

As for the scientific quality, there are two federal appellate cases that merit consideration. Let me summarize each, and relate the judgments to mental health testimony.

First, in *Frye v. United States* (1923), the court indicated that scientific evidence is required to have an underlying scientific principle that is sufficiently established to gain general acceptance in the particular professional field. For about 75 years, the *Frye* test dominated this issue, although it was not applied to social scientific evidence until the mid-1970s (Berger, 1994).

Second, in *Daubert v. Merrell Dow Pharmaceuticals, Inc.,* (1993), the Supreme Court accepted that scientific knowledge is constantly changing, and emphasized the reliability, relevance, and legal sufficiency of the expert testimony:

> To qualify as scientific knowledge, validation must be provided that the influences or assertions of the expert were derived by the scientific method. *Daubert* substantially expanded the role and function of judges as gatekeepers to make these determinations. Rather than formulate a definitive checklist of factors to assess reliability, the Court offered four guidelines: (1) Is the theory or hypothesis falsifiable or testable? (2) Have the findings been subjected to peer review and publication? (3) Is there a known or potential error rate associated with applications of a theory? (4) Is the technique or methodology in issue generally accepted. (Goodman-Delahaunty, 1997, pp. 127-128)

The *Frye* and *Daubert* tests are the cornerstones upon which expert testimony, including from mental health practitioners, should rest. How these tests are applied varies among jurisdictions; and in child custody legal proceedings, judges are known to differ greatly on how, if at all, either or both of these tests are applied.

In mental health services, a plethora of problems arise from the requisite scientific basis. Many opinions expressed in legal cases by mental health practitioners seem to come from their personal experiences, values, and beliefs, not from a scholarly or behavioral science basis.

Especially upsetting for child custody cases, courts seem to seldom challenge the academic and research basis for expert testimony from a mental health practitioner:

> Given psychology's and psychiatry's reliance on unsubstantiated theory, the unreliability of diagnostic classifications, the biases of clinical judgment, and the enormous flaws of psychological tests, one can legitimately argue that psychologists and psychiatrists rarely assist a trier of fact to understand issues or evidence that might otherwise be overlooked without their input. Rather than assist courts with such matters, psychologists and psychiatrists too often impose the erroneous thinking of their own professional convictions on judges and juries alike. (Campbell, 1994, p. 71)

This means that inadequately substantiated expert testimony by the mental health practitioner is potentially an abuse of professionalism.

➜ *Guideline: The mental health practitioner should eschew imposition of their personal experiences, values, and beliefs that lack scholarly and behavioral science basis, and guard against professional convictions that are based on erroneous (nonscientific) thinking.*

If opinions from mental health practitioners have dubious reliability and validity vis-à-vis child custody issues, two questions must be asked. First, why are mental health professionals relied upon in child custody legal proceedings, especially for assessment information? Second, why would a court act in this manner?

The answer to the first question may come from the highly subjective nature of child custody determinations: "Judges may give credence to psychological testimony as a means of escaping the frustrations of attempting to reach the 'correct' result in a difficult case" (Okpaku, 1976, p. 1145). In other words, there is a legal grappling for a rationale for interfering in family relations, and society's designated guardians of psychosocial resources, mental health practitioners, are thought to have the best available voices about the issues.

The answer to the second question may come from the human nature of the trier of fact. Even though mental health information is not often viewed as having more than a modicum of scientific status, the judge typically wants expert testimony to justify his or her answer to the ultimate legal questions. Pragmatically, if a trial judge makes a child custody determination according to the expert testimony of a credible mental health practitioner, there is slight likelihood of the matter being reversed on appeal. As one judge told me, "The number of reversals a judge experiences is his or her report card, which will be read by all the members of the bar and by other judges."

Despite wanting expert testimony in general, judges do not always give high rankings to the opinions expressed by mental health practitioners or attribute significant influence to social science readings and workshops. Also, judges admit to only occasionally relying on the opinions of mental health practitioners in child custody disputes (less frequently than for other legal matters) (Melton et al., 1997).

On the question about the relevance of mental health research to child custody per se, Melton et al. (1997) allege: "*Mental health professionals may have little expertise that is directly relevant to custody disputes*" (p. 483), and conclude:

> Indeed, there is probably no forensic question on which overreaching by mental health professionals has been so common and so egregious. Besides lacking scientific validity, such opinions have often been based on clinical data that are, on their face, irrelevant to the legal questions in dispute. (p. 484)

Despite their negative allegations, Melton et al. (1997) accept that mental health practitioners can be useful to the court: "Clinical impressions about alliances and conflicts within the family and their bases might present judges with a useful framework for consideration of which child goes where" (p. 485). They do, however, impose a limitation on the role of the mental health practitioner, namely: "Child and family clinicians are likely to be efficient and effective gatherers of facts for the court, even when they are not able to add opinions based on specialized knowledge about the implications of those facts" (p. 485). While skilled at collecting information that will be useful to the judge, there is inadequate behavioral science research to allow the mental health practitioner to offer opinions about the meaning of the information.

➜ *Guideline: The mental health practitioner should avoid opinions that are based on clinical data that are irrelevant to the legal questions in dispute, and emphasize being a fact finder or reporter of descriptive information to the court about the persons, alliances, and conflicts within the child's postdivorce family systems.*

It is important to recognize the distinction between being a "fact finder" (e.g., the person who presents factual and descriptive information to the court) versus being an "expert opinion-giver" (e.g., the person who opines about the issues associated with the ultimate legal questions, such as which parent should have primary residential custody and what should be the visitation schedule). In child custody cases, some mental health practitioners are irresponsibly prone to become an "expert opinion-giver," and try to opine about issues thought to be associated with or even answer the ultimate legal question, "Which parent should have custody?" Too often, they seem unperturbed by the lack of scholarly and behavioral science information upon which their expert testimony rests: "Some clinicians (perhaps most) decide nevertheless to testify to what is called the 'ultimate legal question' " (Grisso, 1998, p. 252). Given this irresponsibility, it is no small wonder that so many ethical, regulatory, and legal complaints against mental health practitioners emanate from child custody cases.

Expert testimony by a mental health practitioner that goes beyond a reasonable scholarly and behavioral science basis is unprofessional. When queried about why they would issue an opinion that is not adequately based on scholarship or behavioral science, mental health practitioners commonly give two responses: "Someone has to do it, and I am the best choice to state the opinion," and "The judge ordered me to testify, including answering the ultimate legal question." In the name of professionalism, it is appropriate to counter with: "Two wrongs do not make a right!"

The mental health practitioner should never issue nonprofessional opinions in reports or testimony. Rather, the opinions should reach the following standard: "(a) construct validity of the theories and methodological techniques relied upon; (b) an evaluation of whether the proffered testimony is based upon an acceptable application of the underlying scientific literature; and (c) whether the 'expert' in question has the training, knowledge and experience to utilize the techniques and interpret their results within the context of the underlying theory" (Golding, 1992, p. 255).

At this point, it should be obvious that the scholarly and behavioral science information available and used to formulate expert testimony in child custody cases will have major, perhaps professionally fatal, limitations; yet society is still willing to overlook the shortcomings, and welcome mental health practitioners into the courtroom. The reason is clear-cut: "While social science cannot guarantee that a particular judge has made the 'right' decision in a particular case, social science data and expertise can provide an additional source of information and an additional perspective on what, in all the circumstances and in light of judicial discretion, appears to be in a child's best interests" (Rohman et al., 1987, p. 61). In other words, opinions from mental health practitioners gird judicial decision making, even if it is merely the expert's title that gives the opinion weight.

The foregoing leads Litwack, Gerber, and Fenster (1979-1980) to say that unless there are fixed rules for making custody determinations, a prediction will be necessary; and although mental health professionals cannot issue predictions with anything close to absolute accuracy, the expert testimony will at least provide information to the court that will presumably "increase, however slightly, the accuracy of the prediction the court must make" (p. 283). Stated bluntly, society has concluded that experts are needed in custody proceedings, and public policy and law have accorded authority, even if the opinions are not significantly better than would be offered by a nonprofessional source.

➔ *Guideline: To preserve professionalism, the mental health practitioner must conscientiously try to reconcile the qualitative limitations of mental health information pertaining to child custody issues with society's endorsement of participation for the sake of pragmatic expediency.*

BEING IN A DEPOSITION

In the preceding chapter, coping with a subpoena to obtain mental health records was discussed; and it was noted that the mental health practitioner should view a subpoena as a positive legal tool because it indicates cooperation with legal process and contradicts any notion of advocacy. Moving further, subpoena power can also be used to compel a deposition of the mental health practitioner. Both the mental health records and the transcript of the deposition may potentially be used as exhibits or admissible evidence.

By definition, the statements made in a deposition by the mental health practitioner are not testimony per se. Consider the following definition for a deposition:

> A sworn statement given before a court reporter outside the court setting. In a deposition, the opposing counsel has the opportunity to discover what you plan to testify to at a later date or at trial. Depositions are sometimes taken in lieu of your appearance at a trial. In these instances, you will be questioned and cross-examined as if you were in court, and a transcription of the proceedings will be read into evidence at the actual trial, just as if you were there to testify in person. Some jurisdictions now allow video depositions in place of live testimony. These are taken beforehand and then actually shown to the judge or jury at the trial. (Weikel & Hughes, 1993, p. 4)

Every jurisdiction has its unique set of plentiful rules that apply to the taking of a deposition. Also, the mental health practitioner has little leeway for personal preferences to govern the deposition, such as whether it will be in lieu of a courtroom testimony.

The primary purpose of the deposition is to provide an opportunity for the opposing attorney (the one who will likely find the mental health practitioner's testimony contradictory to the legal interests of his or her particular client) to learn the strengths and weaknesses inherent to the mental health practitioner's professional qualifications and testimony. Therefore, the opposing attorney will likely probe into the vulnerability of the mental health practitioner's credentials, experiences, and personal life, as well as collect information that will allow assessment of the breadth and depth of the expert testimony. The latter is where the scholarly and behavioral science basis for the expert testimony will become an issue.

Sometimes the "friendly" attorney (the one who will likely find the mental health practitioner's testimony to be supportive of the legal interests of his or her particular client) will, after the opposing attorney has finished, ask a few follow-up questions. When this happens, it is seldom to convince either the opposing attorney or the trier of fact in the future of anything. Rather, the intention is to clarify a response made by the mental health practitioner, in order to buttress the credibility of the testimony. For example, if a mental health practitioner's answer suggests flawed reasoning, the attorney may decide, rather than leaving an open door for an in-depth cross-examination of the matter during the trial, to clarify the response to demonstrate to the opposing attorney that the reasoning is flawless.

The deposition is not an opportunity for the mental health practitioner to win or lose the case for either of the parties. In a deposition, perhaps the foremost error made by a mental health practitioner is trying to persuade the opposing counsel of the correct outcome. If the outcome advocated by the mental health practitioner is not fully supportive of the legal interests of the opposing attorney's client, the mental health practitioner has inadvertently and naively "given all of the ammunition to the enemy." In other words, the mental health practitioner has revealed all of his or her ideas, beliefs, interpretations, opinions, and recommendations, thereby allowing the opposing attorney to seek out counterbalancing evidence prior to the trial.

In responding to questions during the deposition, the answers should be brief and to the point of the question. There is no responsibility or duty for the mental health practitioner to flesh out the answer. The only obligation is to answer the question, which should be done honestly and succinctly. Generally, the less said the better; that is, the more that is spoken, the more information the opposing counsel will have to potentially impeach (i.e., discredit) the expert testimony by the mental health practitioner.

➜ *Guideline: In a deposition, the mental health practitioner should answer all questions honestly and succinctly.*

➜ *Guideline: In a deposition, the mental health practitioner should remember that the occasion is not intended to convince the attorneys of anything.*

If either of the attorneys fails to ask a question that the mental health practitioner believes is significant and relevant, the mental health practitioner should not raise the issue. Assuring the quality of the lawyering is not within the role definition for the mental health practitioner.

→ *Guideline: The mental health practitioner should not supply answers to questions that were not asked by an attorney.*

The mental health practitioner should not try to second-guess the intention that underlies a question from either of the attorneys; the same applies to questions that were not asked. Stated differently, the answer to a question should not be structured to try to ward off any legal tactic by the opposing attorney at a later date.

→ *Guideline: The mental health practitioner should not speculate about why a question was or was not asked; to do so would be venturing inappropriately into the realm of legal strategy.*

At the risk of repetition, the deposition is for the sole benefit of the attorney who has subpoenaed the mental health practitioner. The mental health practitioner has no responsibility or duty other than to give straightforward answers. The mental health practitioner owes nothing more to the client who will potentially benefit the most from the expert testimony.

At the personal level, the mental health practitioner should answer all questions in an unemotional manner. Even questions that are clearly intended to attack the mental health practitioner's professional and personal qualities should result in a dispassionate response.

Some attorneys purposefully try to upset the mental health practitioner by probing into his or her personal life: "Cross-examination attorneys will use substantive and psychological means to gain control over witnesses" (Brodsky, 1991, p. 139). I remember one attorney who asked the unmarried mental health practitioner how many men had slept in her house in the past 2 years, and another wanted to know if the mental health practitioner had ever used marijuana.

→ *Guideline: The mental health practitioner should respond to all questions, even those that are clearly intended to attack the mental health practitioner's professional and personal qualities, in a dispassionate manner.*

It is feasible that certain personal questions are relevant and material to the mental health practitioner's involvement in the child custody case (e.g., "Have you ever not had primary residential custody of one of your children?"), but more often than not, the purpose is an attempt to control the mental health practitioner by intimidation. I remember one attorney who probed unmercifully into the custody battle that a mental health practitioner had engaged in with an ex-spouse.

When deposition questions seem to be too personal or for the purpose of intimidation, the mental health practitioner should calmly respond: "With great respect for the legal system, I decline to respond to your question." If the opposing attorney then presses for or commands an answer, the mental health practitioner, retaining composure, should respond: "Again with great respect for the legal system, I decline to respond to your question, and formally request that this question be certified to the honorable judge for a ruling on whether or not I have to answer it." At that point, the opposing attorney is legally obligated to submit a motion to the court asking for a ruling. If this occurs, which seldom happens, the mental health practitioner should ask to be "noticed for the hearing," meaning that the mental health practitioner wishes to appear before the court and state why, in the opinion of the mental health practitioner, the question is improper (e.g., "an invasion of my right to privacy, and is not relevant and material to the legal issues before this honorable court"). Note that jurisdictions may vary on a deponent's refusing to answer a question, which raises the possibility that some child custody cases may necessitate that mental health practitioners seek legal counsel or even have legal counsel present during the deposition (or trial).

 ➔ *Guideline: Questions that seem to be an inappropriate assault on the mental health practitioner's personal rights (e.g., privacy) should be countered by a formal request that the question be certified to the court for a ruling on whether it does or does not have to be answered.*

In regard to intimidation, a few attorneys believe the approach of choice for dealing with a mental health practitioner is to be hostile-aggressive. Some of these attorneys have admitted that they do it, not because it will produce positive results, but because they think the hostile-aggressive approach will impress their clients.

When an attorney becomes profane or vulgar, the mental health practitioner should respond: "I was under the impression that a deposition was to be conducted with respect for the deponent and with the decorum required in the courtroom—therefore, I respectfully request that you cease and desist from the rude, crude, and lewd language that you are using." If the attorney ill-advisedly persists, the mental health practitioner should terminate the deposition.

If an attorney is clearly insulting, denigrating, abrasive, and abusive by language or deed directed at the mental health practitioner, such misconduct should not be tolerated. Although jurisdictions vary a bit in their ethics codes, most (if not all) have statements that require an attorney to show reasonable respect and politeness to any person in the legal proceedings, and some ethics codes specify that the attorney is to be respectful and polite to nonparties (like the mental health practitioner who will be giving expert testimony). When an attorney transgresses in this manner, the mental health practitioner should consider contacting the ethics office of the state bar.

→ *Guideline: The mental health practitioner should not tolerate any disrespect or rude, crude, or lewd language by an attorney during a deposition (or in any other situation).*

A most important guideline is that in any confrontation with an attorney, the mental health practitioner should remain calm and unemotional. The mental health practitioner should simply shift into a "therapeutic modality," and conceptualize the attorney as being like a client in a therapeutic exchange. For example, the mental health practitioner can think, "If I had an abrasive person act in therapy the way this attorney is acting, how would I respond?" This approach should lead to the desired calm and unemotional response.

In confrontive circumstances, everything that is said should be taken down by the court reporter. If the attorney says to the court reporter, "Let's go off the record" (meaning, "don't take down what is going to be said"), the mental health practitioner should object and insist that the exchange be "on the record" (meaning, "I want this taken down by the court reporter"). If there is ever an impasse on issues of this kind, the mental health practitioner must have the backbone to stand firm and exit the deposition if necessary. Immediately afterward, the mental health practitioner should write out a description of what happened; contemporaneously made notes are well received in the legal system. The transcript of and the notes about the unfortunate exchange would likely prove to be useful for either countering a motion of contempt of court filed against the mental health practitioner, or pursuing sanctions against the attorney by a motion to the court or a complaint to the state bar.

→ *Guideline: When in an unfortunate confrontation with an attorney, the mental health practitioner should remain calm and unemotional, get the exchange recorded by a court reporter, and immediately thereafter, the mental health practitioner should write out a description of what transpired.*

BEING ON THE WITNESS STAND

This book has offered considerable information, including guidelines, relevant to giving expert testimony in child custody cases. This section brings all of that information into focus. Also, the information set forth in the preceding section on being deposed has distinct relevance to expert testimony from the witness stand, and should be generalized accordingly.

→ *Guideline: In a trial, the mental health practitioner is not expected to win or lose the case, and should not attempt to persuade the trier of fact of an answer to ultimate legal questions.*

Entering the courtroom, the mental health practitioner may find the august atmosphere and being asked for information and opinions exhilarating. Caution is needed to avoid undue or inappropriate responses—delusions of self-aggrandizement must not be allowed.

As in other stages of a child custody case, the mental health practitioner's mode of operation during testimony should adhere strictly to the designated role and functions. At the testimony stage, the designated role is defined by the reason for allowing the mental health practitioner into the case in the first place. The reason is stated succinctly in Federal Rule of Evidence 702: "If scientific, technical or other specialized knowledge will assist the trier of fact to understand the evidence or to determine a fact in issue, a witness qualified as an expert by knowledge, skill, experience, training or education, may testify thereto in the form of an opinion or otherwise." As has been said before, the mental health practitioner is, simply put, in the legal proceedings to assist the trier of fact, the judge (or in certain kinds of cases, the jury).

When giving testimony, the mental health practitioner's function is to provide information in an educative fashion. This teaching function underlies McElhaney's (1997) recommendation for selecting an expert witness:

> Credibility is at the heart of every case. And the teacher is a fundamental symbol of credibility in our society. So look for someone who loves to explain things to other people, who feels natural with a piece of chalk in hand, who enjoys showing others how things work. (p. 82)

There are, of course, many mental health practitioners who are excellent clinicians, but poor educators (and vice versa).

→ *Guideline: To be effective at child custody testimony, the mental health practitioner should cultivate educative skills.*

It has been mentioned before and it deserves to be mentioned again: The mental health practitioner is not in the legal proceedings to become either a legal advocate or a quasi-judge. From analyzing ethics, regulatory, and legal complaints, I believe that two of the most frequent situations that lead to a complaint are that the mental health practitioner is perceived as (a) a legal advocate for one party more than the other or (b) an advocate of a legal issue that is thought to be to the detriment of the complainant. Persuading the trier of fact of the reliability and validity of a point of information should not be confused with promoting a particular legal determination.

→ *Guideline: The mental health practitioner should limit the persuasive dimension of testimony to educating the trier of fact to understand, appreciate, and accept the scholarly and behavioral science basis for the testimony; stated differently, the mental health practitioner should not advocate or attempt to persuade the trier of fact to adopt an answer for an ultimate legal question.*

Testimony must, as has been repeatedly stated for other functions, derive from and should be limited to scholarly and behavioral science information. Shapiro (1991) pinpoints the problem: "A pit-fall to be avoided is the attempt to extend a sound clinical or psychological judgment to an unfounded generalization" (p. 224).

As an example of overgeneralizing or overreaching from what would otherwise be a reasonable scholarly or behavioral science viewpoint, it is all too common for a mental health practitioner to opine answers, sometimes in response to a request from the judge, for the ultimate legal questions: "Which parent should have primary residential custody?" and "What should be the visitation schedule?" The only correct answer to both of these questions would be: "Your honor, the scholarly and behavioral science information available for my mental health discipline does not provide adequate basis for my formulating an answer; were I to answer the question, I respectfully submit that my opinion would not be an expert opinion, and it would potentially intrude on the providence of this honorable court."

Although it may be tempting to respond with an answer, the mental health practitioner must accept that there is, in fact, inadequate research on many ultimate legal issues, especially in child custody cases. As an exemplary exercise, the reader should try to identify research studies in the professional literature in his or her mental health discipline that provide empirical evidence that would allow even an opinion with a reasonable degree of certainty about who should have primary residential custody and what should be the visitation schedule. Of special concern, research on determining primary residential custody and the visitation schedule by data from psychological tests is inadequate.

The mental health practitioner is, of course, learned about human behavior. This knowledge can lead to an informed opinion about certain matters clearly associated with the ultimate legal questions, which can appropriately be manifested in an information-giving manner. For example, research on child development would supply answers to questions about the needs and vulnerabilities of a child at a given age, the effect of inconsistent (e.g., overly emotionalized) parenting, the benefits of sibling relations, and so on. The latter does not reach, however, to supplying the answers for the ultimate legal questions. That task remains for the judge.

Although some jurisdictions allow expert witnesses to address or give opinions about the ultimate legal questions, this does not provide a justification for mental health practitioners to engage in the practice. When consideration is given to the lack of empirical research and the role and functions that are endorsed by public policy and laws, it seems that professional ethics and standards preclude mental health practitioners giving answers to the ultimate legal questions. Without a substantial amount of scholarly and behavioral science information, answering the ultimate legal questions by a mental health practitioner would potentially be an abuse of professionalism.

Answers for the ultimate legal questions should come only from the trier of fact—the sole source truly authorized and granted immunity by society. The mental health practitioner who offers answers for the ultimate legal questions would be left with a significant risk of ethical, regulatory, and licensing complaints.

→ *Guideline: When deciding whether or not to issue an opinion about an ultimate legal question, the mental health practitioner should consider the empirical research that, in fact, exists; and without a substantial amount of research directly applicable to the question, the mental health practitioner should readily admit that his or her opinion, although steeped in knowledge about human behavior in general, would not be expert opinion.*

The mental health practitioner who is foolish enough to attempt to guise an opinion as being "expert" when there are inadequate scholarly and behavioral science bases can be impeached in cross-examination. When the expert's testimony is impeached, the likelihood of ethics, regulatory, or legal complaints increases considerably—and deservedly so.

In offering expert testimony for child custody legal proceedings, the mental health practitioner should follow the guidelines set forth in the preceding section on being deposed, and others that can be gleaned from the materials in the earlier chapters. All ideas about expert testimony in child custody cases should be compatible with the accepted role and purposes, and the educative function.

Turning to guidelines specific to child custody legal proceedings, one of the most blatant violations of professional ethics and standards occurs when the mental health practitioner states clinically oriented opinions about someone with whom there has been little or no meaningful contact. Psychologists are to "provide written or oral forensic reports or testimony of the psychological characteristics of an individual only after they have conducted an

examination of the individual adequate to support their statements or conclusions" (American Psychological Association, 1992,
p. 1610). In addition, forensic psychologists are cautioned to "avoid
giving written or oral evidence about the psychological characteristics of particular individuals when they have not had an opportunity to conduct an examination of the individual adequate to the
scope of the statements, opinions, or conclusions to be issued"
(Committee on Ethical Guidelines for Forensic Psychologists, 1991,
p. 663). The American Psychological Association's (1994) child
custody guidelines provide further clarification of this issue:

> **The psychologist does not give any opinion regarding
> the psychological functioning of any individual who has
> not been personally evaluated.** This guideline, however,
> does not preclude the psychologist from reporting what an
> evaluated individual (such as the parent or child) has stated
> or from addressing theoretical issues or hypothetical ques-
> tions, so long as the limited basis of the information is noted.
> (p. 679)

Although not stated as specifically in the ethics codes for the mental health disciplines other than psychology, the standard seems
appropriate for all child custody scenarios. In upholding this standard, the mental health practitioner is promoting both quality care
for the parties and others (including society), as well as gaining risk
management to ward off an ethical, regulatory, or legal complaint.

→ *Guideline: The mental health practitioner should only testify
about persons with whom there has been direct and sufficient
contacts adequate to meet the prevailing professional ethics
and standards for the purpose (e.g., evaluation); and the mental health practitioner should make clear the professional and
empirical limits of a response about theoretical issues or hypothetical questions.*

When formulating responses during testimony, the mental
health practitioner should not hesitate to respectfully decline to answer a question: "When you truly don't know, say so" (Brodsky,
1991, p. 175). During testimony, it is appropriate for the attorney to
attempt to elicit as much supportive information as possible from
the mental health practitioner. This is in keeping with legal advocacy.

On occasion, I have declined to answer a question posed by an attorney or a judge because of inadequate scholarly and behavioral science bases, only to have the judge say something like: "I realize it is speculation, Dr. Woody, but I would appreciate your responding to the question anyway." In those instances, there may be no certain way out of the dilemma, but all mental health practitioners must politely assert that to speculate in that manner would potentially violate the prevailing professional ethics and standards. In the end, the judge could, of course, order a response, but at least it would have been properly couched with limitations.

➔ ***Guideline:*** *The mental health practitioner should readily admit limits of knowledge and avoid speculating beyond what would be supported by reasonable scholarly and behavioral science information; and if ordered by the court to respond beyond the limits of knowledge, the mental health practitioner should state reservations and limitations, including that the response should not be deemed "professional" or "expert."*

As a final caveat, in child custody legal proceedings, there is no room for a mental health practitioner to become a "crusader for justice" or a "super hero." Stated differently, the duty to pursue legal advocacy is assigned to the attorneys and the triers of fact. Attorneys are on the lookout for mental health practitioners who "bring their own problems to court disguised as objective, scientific opinion" (R. S. Greenbaum & D. A. Greenbaum, 1998, p. 12). As Brodksy (1991) put it: "A witness's self-centeredness about the importance of personal testimony can serve as blinders that interfere with clarity, self-assurance, and nondefensiveness" (p. 181). Here again, much like testifying without reasonable scholarly and behavioral science bases, the mental health practitioner who becomes an advocate for an outcome, which may have little or no relevance to the parties and their children in the particular case, incurs great risk of an ethical, regulatory, and legal complaint.

Critiquing the Testimony of Colleagues

Earlier mention was made of the "Battle of the Experts." Similarly, it is common for an attorney to hire a mental health practitioner to critique the testimony being offered by another mental health practitioner who will be testifying against the interests of the attorney's client.

With precautions, critiquing the testimony provided by other mental health practitioners (colleagues) can be appropriate, especially if the colleagues seem to have transgressed: "Psychologists are concerned about the ethical compliance of their colleagues' scientific and professional conduct" (American Psychological Association, 1992, p. 1599). With or without transgression, the child custody guidelines from the American Psychological Association (1994) acknowledge the propriety of critiquing others: "A psychologist may be asked to critique the assumptions and methodology of the assessment of another mental health professional" (p. 679). For example, it would be potentially appropriate for a mental health practitioner (assuming competency) to: provide scholarly information that contradicted what a colleague said; or offer opinions about the standards maintained in mental health services, which might indicate shortcomings on the part of the colleague.

When critiquing a colleague, the mental health practitioner should remain mindful of the welfare of all concerned, and avoid unnecessarily negative, unjust, or hurtful responses. The principle of "do no harm" is axiomatic to all mental health disciplines.

➜ *Guideline: When critiquing the testimony of a colleague, the mental health practitioner should guard against negative, unjust, and hurtful responses.*

The primary objective for a critique of the testimony by colleagues is to strengthen the judicial process: "Forensic psychologists are aware that their essential role as expert to the court is to assist the trier of fact to understand the evidence or to determine a fact in issue" (Committee on Ethical Guidelines for Forensic Psychologists, 1991, p. 665). Although the attorney may recruit the critic to advance the legal interests of his or her particular client, the mental health practitioner should not be duped into becoming an advocate for that party. The objective of the critique is not to "win the case" for anyone.

➜ *Guideline: When critiquing the testimony of a colleague, the mental health practitioner should respond only according to the objective of assisting the trier of fact to understand the evidence or to determine a fact in issue.*

When critiquing and presumably refuting (at least in part) the opinions expressed by other mental health professionals, the mental health practitioner should always consider "opposing" mental health practitioners to be professional colleagues. Therefore, the mental health practitioner should, at all times, be "honest, fair, and respectful of others" (American Psychological Association, 1992, p. 1599); and psychologists are also told: "In their work-related activities, psychologists respect the rights of others to hold values, attitudes, and opinions that differ from their own" (p. 1601). The foregoing are apt standards for all mental health practitioners.

When offering critiques of other witnesses, the mental health practitioner should be especially careful to not second-guess clinical opinions. Remember that substantial and direct contact must underlie any opinion about psychological functioning, regardless of professional discipline. For example, the Code of Conduct for the Association of State and Provincial Psychology Boards (ASPPB; 1991) holds that: "A psychologist rendering a formal professional opinion about a person, for example about the fitness of a parent in a custody hearing, shall not do so without direct and substantial professional contact with or a formal assessment of that person" (pp. 8-9).

If a treating therapist or evaluator testifies about psychological functioning, the critic's testimony should be limited to addressing the scholarly and behavioral science bases that were or were not apparent in the testimony by the colleague. For clarification, psychologists are not precluded "from addressing theoretical issues or hypothetical questions, so long as the limited basis of the information is noted" (American Psychological Association, 1994, p. 679).

→ *Guideline: When critiquing the testimony of a treating therapist or evaluator, the mental health practitioner should address the scholarly and behavioral science bases that were or were not apparent in the testimony by the colleague, and should avoid any second-guessing of clinical opinions offered by the treating therapist or evaluator.*

In child custody cases, unique problems arise when the treating therapist or evaluator is asked (perhaps ordered by the court) to critique the testimony of the mental health practitioner hired to critique in turn the treating therapist's or evaluator's testimony. Although multiple roles are not patently inappropriate, testifying in a child custody case as a treating therapist or custody evaluator might restrict accepting an additional role of critiquing other professional witnesses.

If the critic challenges the testimony of the treating therapist or evaluator, it would seem that the treating therapist or evaluator should be able to rehabilitate his or her testimony by elaboration of the scholarly and behavioral science bases for the treatment or evaluation framework. It might be inappropriate, however, for the treating therapist or evaluator to enter into a "Battle of the Experts" about issues that are beyond the treatment or evaluation per se.

➔ *Guideline: The mental health practitioner who has served as treating therapist or evaluator for a child custody case should avoid testifying about issues that are beyond the treatment or evaluation per se.*

BECOMING PREPARED FOR EXPERT TESTIMONY

When anyone asks me, "How can I learn to be an effective witness in legal cases," I usually respond: "Start studying textbooks and articles that pertain to the legal process and forensic mental health services." I recommend reading, *Testifying in Court: Guidelines and Maxims for the Expert Witness* (Brodsky, 1991) and *Psychological Evaluations for the Courts* (Melton et al., 1997). I also encourage the would-be witness to become familiar with the relevant laws of the jurisdiction. To avoid relying on television simulations of legal proceedings, such as "Judge Judy" and others, I encourage observing actual cases involving testimony by mental health practitioners. Contacting a mental health colleague who is known to provide expert testimony may produce an opportunity to tag along to the courtroom. Finally, there is no substitute for extensive formal and continuing education, and supervision from a wise forensic mental health practitioner.

➔ *Guideline: Before working in child custody cases, the mental health practitioner should obtain knowledge of relevant legal principles, the laws of the jurisdiction, and the professional ethics and standards, which will likely involve formal and continuing education, observation, and supervision.*

ADOPTING AN APPROPRIATE MINDSET

In this book, I have offered many suggestions, guidelines, and caveats intended to shape the development of an appropriate professional and personal mindset for testimony in child custody legal proceedings. Obviously, offering testimony in a child custody case is a complex and risky undertaking.

I have encountered numerous mental health practitioners who, because of the trials and tribulations inflicted by managed care, consider forensic services to be a profitable role. Child custody cases seem to have a magnetic appeal for many of these dissatisfied mental health practitioners. Without adequate preparation, they plunge into child custody cases, only to face ethical, regulatory, and legal complaints because of the nature of the specialty and ineffective practice. For some, instead of being a "practice builder," forensic services became a "practice buster." Forensic services require special preparation, which spans education, training, and personal qualities.

Any notion that forensic services in general and child custody cases in particular can create assured success and professional distinction should be dispelled immediately. Any belief that involvement in child custody cases will allow the mental health practitioner to accomplish great things through advocacy of the welfare and rights of children, which has considerable humanitarian appeal, should be tempered with recognition of the limits placed on the accepted role and functions, as well as concern about the concomitant risk of ethical, regulatory, and legal complaints.

➜ *Guideline: The mental health practitioner should recognize that forensic service: requires extensive formal academic and experiential preparation; is highly demanding for expertise and personal fortitude; carries financial uncertainty; and imposes a high risk of ethical, regulatory, and legal complaints.*

As one seasoned mental health practitioner said, "I need a new income stream for my private practice and would like to do forensic work, but I really doubt I could put up with the intense scrutiny and control to which I would be subjected by attorneys, not to mention the risk of a complaint." What comes to mind is the old adage, "Many are called, but few are chosen."

Ending on the proverbial positive note, providing forensic mental health services can be highly rewarding. As with any endeavor, however, the reward will have to be earned by hard work and investment of resources. There is no guarantee of success. Nonetheless, there is the opportunity to promote the best interests of children, and to do so within the context of a healthy and constructive family life. The fabric of our society is, of course, critically dependent on the protection and cultivation of children and their families. The legal system welcomes and needs high-quality mental health services, especially in child custody cases.

➔ *Guideline: The mental health practitioner should recognize that there is no guarantee of success for forensic services and there are extensive demands and risks; but there is also the potential for making a significant contribution to society through participating in efforts to assure the best interests of children.*

REFERENCES

Ackerman, M. J., & Ackerman, M. C. (1996). Child custody evaluation practices: A 1996 survey of psychologists. *Family Law Quarterly, 30*(3), 565-586.

Ackerman, M. J., & Ackerman, M. C. (1997). Custody evaluation practices: A survey of experienced professionals (revisited). *Professional Psychology, 28*(2), 137-145.

Ackerman, M. J., & Schoendorf, K. (1992). *Ackerman-Schoendorf Scales for Parent Evaluation of Custody (ASPECT)*. Los Angeles: Western Psychological Services.

American Association for Marriage and Family Therapy. (1998). *AAMFT Code of Ethics*. Washington, DC: Author.

American Psychological Association. (1992). Ethical principles of psychologists and code of conduct. *American Psychologist, 47*(12), 1597-1611.

American Psychological Association. (1993). Record keeping guidelines. *American Psychologist, 48*(9), 984-986.

American Psychological Association. (1994). Guidelines for child custody evaluations in divorce proceedings. *American Psychologist, 49*(7), 677-680.

American Psychological Association. (1996a). Statement on the disclosure of test data. *American Psychologist, 51*(6), 644-648.

American Psychological Association. (1996b). Strategies for private practitioners coping with subpoenas or compelled testimony for client records or test data. *Professional Psychology, 27*(3), 245-251.

Arkowitz, H. (1992). Integrative theories of therapy. In D. Freedheim (Ed.), *The History of Psychotherapy: A Century of Change* (pp. 261-303). Washington, DC: American Psychological Association.

Association of State and Provincial Psychology Boards. (1991). *ASPPB Code of Conduct.* Montgomery, AL: Author.

Bennett, B. E., Bryant, B. K., VandenBos, G. R., & Greenwood, A. (1990). *Professional Liability and Risk Management.* Washington, DC: American Psychological Association.

Berger, M. A. (1994). Procedural paradigms for applying the *Daubert* test. *Minnesota Law Review, 78,* 1345-1385.

Bogolub, E. B. (1995). *Helping Families Through Divorce: An Eclectic Approach.* New York: Springer.

Botein, B. (1952). *Trial Judge.* New York: Simon and Schuster.

Brammer, L. M., Shostrom, E. L., & Abrego, P. J. (1989). *Therapeutic Psychology: Fundamentals of Counseling and Psychotherapy* (5th ed.). Englewood Cliffs, NJ: Prentice-Hall.

Bricklin, B. (1984). *Bricklin Perceptual Scales.* Furlong, PA: Village.

Bricklin, B. (1998). Sequence of steps and critical assessment targets of a comprehensive custody evaluation. In G. P. Koocher, J. C. Norcross, & S. S. Hill, III (Eds.), *Psychologists' Desk Reference* (pp. 499-502). New York: Oxford University Press.

Brinson, P., & Hess, K. D. (1987). Mediating domestic law issues. In I. B. Weiner & A. K. Hess (Eds.), *Handbook of Forensic Psychology* (pp. 86-127). New York: John Wiley.

Brock, G. W., & Barnard, C. P. (1999). *Procedures in Marriage and Family Therapy* (3rd ed.). Needham Heights, MA: Allyn and Bacon.

Brodsky, S. L. (1991). *Testifying in Court: Guidelines and Maxims for the Expert Witness.* Washington, DC: American Psychological Association.

Brooks-Gunn, J., & Duncan, G. J. (1998). Poor families, poor outcomes: The well-being of children and youth. *Family Psychologist, 14*(2), 16-19.

Burke, C. A. (1995). Until death do us part: An exploration into confidentiality following the death of a client. *Professional Psychology, 26*(3), 278-280.

Campbell, T. W. (1994). Challenging psychologists and psychiatrists as expert witnesses. *Michigan Bar Journal, 73*(1), 68-72.

Committee on Ethical Guidelines for Forensic Psychologists. (1991). Specialty guidelines for forensic psychologists. *Law and Human Behavior, 15*(6), 655-665.

Committee on Professional Practice and Standards. (1998). *Guidelines for Psychological Evaluations in Child Protection Matters.* Washington, DC: American Psychological Association.

Corsini, R. J. (Ed.). (1981). *Handbook of Innovative Psychotherapies.* New York: John Wiley.

Crosby-Currie, C. A. (1996). Children's involvement in contested custody cases: Practices and experiences of legal and mental health professionals. *Law and Human Behavior, 20*(3), 289-310.

Daubert v. Merrell Dow Pharmaceuticals, Inc., 113 S.Ct. 2786 (1993).

Dickson, D. T. (1995). *Law in the Health and Human Services.* New York: The Free Press (Simon & Schuster).

Donovan, D. M., & Chaney, E. F. (1985). Alcoholic relapse prevention and intervention: Models and methods. In G. A. Marlatt & J. R. Gordon (Eds.), *Relapse Prevention* (pp. 351-416). New York: Guilford.

Ellsworth, P., & Levy, R. (1969). Legislative reform of child custody adjudication: An effort to rely on social science data in formulating legal policies. *Law and Society Review, 4,* 167-233.

Engler, J., & Quinn, K. (1998). On the trail of deadbeat parents. *Michigan Bar Journal, 77*(3), 276-279.

Fanshel, D. (1957). *A Study in Negro Adoption.* New York: Child Welfare League of America.

Feiner, R. D., & Terre, L. (1987). Child custody dispositions and children's adaptation following divorce. In L. A. Weithorn (Ed.), *Psychology and Child Custody Determinations* (pp. 106-153). Lincoln, NE: University of Nebraska Press.

Ford, D. H., & Urban, H. B. (1998). *Contemporary Models of Psychotherapy: A Comparative Analysis* (2nd ed.). New York: John Wiley.

Frye v. United States, 293 F.Supp. 1013 (D.C. Cir. 1923).

Gindes, M. (1995). Competence and training in child custody evaluations. *American Journal of Family Therapy, 2*(3) 273-280.

Goldfried, M. R. (1980). Toward the delineation of therapeutic change principles. *American Psychologist, 35,* 991-999.

Golding, S. L. (1992). Increasing the reliability, validity, and relevance of psychological expert evidence: An introduction to the

Special Issue on Expert Evidence. *Law and Human Behavior,*
16, 253-256.

Goldstein, J., Freud, A., & Solnit, A. J. (1973). *Beyond the Best*
Interests of the Child. New York: The Free Press (Simon &
Schuster).

Goldstein, J., Solnit, A. J., Goldstein, S., & Freud, A. (1996). *The*
Best Interests of the Child: The Least Detrimental Alternative.
New York: The Free Press (Simon & Schuster).

Goodman, G. S., & Hahn, A. (1987). Evaluating eyewitness testimony. In I. B. Weiner & A. K. Hess (Eds.), *Handbook of Foren-*
sic Psychology (pp. 258-292). New York: John Wiley.

Goodman-Delahunty, J. (1997). Forensic psychological expertise
in the wake of *Daubert*. *Law and Human Behavior, 21*(2), 121-
140.

Granello, P. F., & Witmer, J. M. (1998). Standard of care: Potential
implications for the counseling profession. *Journal of Counsel-*
ing and Development, 76(4), 371-380.

Greenbaum, R. S., & Greenbaum, D. A. (1998). Forensic examination of mental health experts in custody, visitation or relocation
conflicts. *Family Law Commentator, 23*(1), 10-12.

Grisso, T. (1998). *Forensic Evaluation of Juveniles*. Sarasota, FL:
Professional Resource Press.

Hayes, S. C. (1987). A contextual approach to therapeutic change.
In N. S. Jacobson (Ed.), *Psychotherapists in Clinical Practice:*
Cognitive and Behavioral Perspectives (pp. 327-387). New York:
Guilford.

Hermann, D. H. J. (1997). *Mental Health and Disability Law*. St.
Paul, MN: West.

Hill, S. S., III. (1998). Client-therapist compatibility. In G. P.
Koocher, J. C. Norcross, & S. S. Hill, III (Eds.), *Psychologists'*
Desk Reference (pp. 197-199). New York: Oxford University
Press.

Jaffe, S. R. (Producer), & Benton, R. (Director). (1979). *Kramer*
Versus Kramer [Film]. (Columbia Pictures)

Keilin, W. G., & Bloom, L. J. (1986). Child custody evaluation practices: A survey of experienced professionals. *Professional Psy-*
chology, 17, 338-346.

Koocher, G. P. (1998). Basic elements of release forms. In G. P.
Koocher, J. C. Norcross, & S. S. Hill, III (Eds.), *Psychologists'*

Desk Reference (pp. 467-469). New York: Oxford University Press.

Kuehnle, K. (1996). *Assessing Allegations of Child Sexual Abuse.* Sarasota, FL: Professional Resource Press.

Kuehnle, K. (1998). Child sexual abuse: Treatment issues. In G. P. Koocher, J. C. Norcross, & S. S. Hill, III (Eds.), *Psychologists' Desk Reference* (pp. 252-256). New York: Oxford University Press.

Lazarus, A. A. (1981). *The Practice of Multimodal Therapy.* New York: McGraw-Hill.

Lazarus, A. A. (1989). *The Practice of Multimodal Therapy* (rev. ed.). Baltimore: Johns Hopkins University Press.

Litwack, T., Gerber, G., & Fenster, A. (1979-1980). The proper role of psychology in child custody disputes. *Journal of Family Law, 18,* 269-300.

Lowery, C. (1981). Child custody decisions in divorce proceedings: A survey of judges. *Professional Psychology, 12,* 492-498.

Maddi, S. R. (1996). *Personality Theories: A Comparative Analysis* (6th ed.). Pacific Grove, CA: Brooks/Cole.

McElhaney, J. W. (1997). Terms of enlightenment: Articulate expert witnesses help jurors visualize facts. *ABA Journal, 83*(5), 82-83.

Melton, G. B., & Lind, E. A. (1982). Procedural justice in family court: Does the adversary model make sense? *Child and Youth Services, 5,* 63-81.

Melton, G. B., Petrila, J., Poythress, N. G., & Slobogin, C. (1997). *Psychological Evaluations for the Court: A Handbook for Mental Health Professionals and Lawyers* (2nd ed.). New York: Guilford.

Meyer v. Nebraska, 262 U.S. 390 (1923).

Miner v. Miner, 11 Ill. 43 (1849).

National Conference of Commissioners on Uniform State Laws. (1971). Uniform Marriage and Divorce Act. *Family Law Quarterly, 6*(1), 106-111.

Norcross, J. C., & Goldfried, M. R. (Eds.). (1992). *Handbook of Psychotherapy Integration.* New York: Basic Books.

Nurcombe, B., & Partlett, B. (1994). *Child Mental Health and the Law.* New York: The Free Press (Macmillan).

Okpaku, S. (1976). Psychology: Impediment or aid in child custody cases? *Rutgers Law Review, 29,* 1117-1153.

Oldershaw, L., & Bagby, R. M. (1997). Children and deception. In R. Rogers (Ed.), *Clinical Assessment of Malingering and Deception* (2nd ed., pp. 153-166). New York: Guilford.

Pierce v. Society of Sisters, 268 U.S. 510 (1925).

Prince v. Massachusetts, 321 U.S. 158 (1944).

Read, J. (1997). Child abuse and psychosis: A literature review and implications for professional practice. *Professional Psychology, 28*(5), 448-456.

Remley, T. P., Jr. (1991). *Preparing for Court Appearances.* Alexandria, VA: American Counseling Association.

Robertson, M. H. (1995). *Psychotherapy Education and Training: An Integrative Perspective.* Madison, CT: International Universities Press.

Robertson, M. H., & Woody, R. H. (1997). *Theories and Methods for Practice of Clinical Psychology.* Madison, CT: International Universities Press.

Rogers, L. C. (1987). The judicial interview with the child. *Louisiana Law Review, 47,* 559-588.

Rohman, L. W., Sales, B. D., & Lou, M. (1987). The best interests of the child in custody disputes. In L. A. Weithorn (Ed.), *Psychology and Child Custody Determinations* (pp. 59-105). Lincoln, NE: University of Nebraska Press.

Ross, K. L. (1999). *State v. Michaels*: A New Jersey Supreme Court ruling with national implications. *Michigan Bar Journal, 78*(1), 32-35.

Scott, E. S., & Emery, R. (1987). Child custody dispute resolution: The adversarial system and divorce mediation. In L. A. Weithorn (Ed.), *Psychology and Child Custody Determinations* (pp. 23-56). Lincoln, NE: University of Nebraska Press.

Scott, E. S., Reppucci, N. D., & Aber, M. (1988). Children's preference in adjudicated custody decisions. *Georgia Law Review, 22,* 1035-1078.

Settle, S. A., & Lowery, C. R. (1982). Child custody decisions: Content analysis of a judicial survey. *Journal of Divorce, 6,* 125-138.

Shapiro, D. L. (1991). *Forensic Psychological Assessment: An Integrative Approach.* Boston: Allyn and Bacon.

Slicker, W. D. (1998). Child testimony. *Florida Bar Journal, 72*(10), 46-49.

Stricker, G. (Chair). (1998, August 15). *Symposium: Ethical Concerns for the '90s*. Paper presented at the annual convention of the American Psychological Association, San Francisco, CA.

Thompson, R. C., Paul, R. (Producers), Bridges, J., & Thompson, R. C. (Directors). (1973). *The Paper Chase*. [Film]. (Fox Pictures)

Wadlington, W. (Ed.). (1995). *Family Law Statutes, Treaties and Legislative Models*. Westbury, NY: Foundation Press.

Wallerstein, J. (1994). Children of divorce: Preliminary report of a ten-year follow-up. *American Journal of Orthopsychiatry, 54*, 444-458.

Wallerstein, J. (1994). Children of divorce: Challenge for the 1990's. *Journal of Jewish Communal Service, 70*, 100-108.

Warshak, R. A. (1992). *The Custody Revolution: The Father Factor and the Motherhood Mystique*. New York: Poseidon Press.

Weikel, W. J., & Hughes, P. R. (1993). *The Counselor as Expert Witness*. Alexandria, VA: American Counseling Association.

Weithorn, L. A. (1987). Psychological consultation in divorce custody litigation: Ethical considerations. In L. A. Weithorn (Ed.), *Psychology and Child Custody Determinations* (pp. 183-209). Lincoln, NE: University of Nebraska Press.

Weithorn, L. A., & Grisso, T. (1987). Psychological evaluations in divorce custody: Problems, principles, and procedures. In L. A. Weithorn (Ed.), *Psychology and Child Custody Determinations* (pp. 157-181). Lincoln, NE: University of Nebraska Press.

White, M., & Epstein, D. (1990). *Narrative Means to Therapeutic Ends*. New York: W. W. Norton.

Woody, R. H. (1971). *Psychobehavioral Counseling and Therapy: Integrating Behavioral and Insight Techniques*. New York: Appleton-Century-Crofts.

Woody, R. H. (1975). *Child Custody Legal Proceedings: An Investigation of Criteria Maintained by Lawyers, Psychiatrists, Psychologists, and Social Workers*. Unpublished Doctor of Science dissertation, University of Pittsburgh's Graduate School of Public Health, Pittsburgh, PA.

Woody, R. H. (1977a). Behavioral science criteria in child custody determinations. *Journal of Marriage and Family Counseling, 3*, 11-18.

Woody, R. H. (1977b). Psychologists in child custody. In B. D. Sales (Ed.), *Psychology in the Legal Process* (pp. 249-267). New York: Spectrum.

Woody, R. H. (1977c). Sexism in child custody decisions. *Personnel and Guidance Journal, 56*, 168-170.

Woody, R. H. (1978). *Getting Custody: Winning the Last Battle of the Marital War*. New York: Macmillan.

Woody, R. H. (1991). *Quality Care in Mental Health Services: Assuring the Best Clinical Services*. San Francisco: Jossey-Bass.

Woody, R. H. (1993). Regulatory equality for clients and psychotherapists. *Voices: The Art and Science of Psychotherapy, 29*(2), 87-92.

Woody, R. H. (1997). *Legally Safe Mental Health Practice*. Madison, CT: International Universities Press (Psychosocial Books).

Woody, R. H. (2000). *Psychological Information: Protecting the Right of Privacy*. Madison, CT: International Universities Press (Psychosocial Books).

Worden, M. (1999). *Family Therapy Basics* (2nd ed.). Pacific Grove, CA: Brooks/Cole.

Wright, R. H. (1981). What to do until the malpractice lawyer comes: A survivor's manual. *American Psychologist, 36*, 1535-1541.

Wyer, M. M., Gaylord, S. J., & Grove, E. T. (1987). The legal context of child custody evaluations. In L. A. Weithorn (Ed.), *Psychology and Child Custody Determinations* (pp. 3-22). Lincoln, NE: University of Nebraska Press.

Zilbach, J. J. (1986). *Young Children in Family Therapy*. New York: Brunner/Mazel.

SUBJECT INDEX

Custody,
    alternating, 38-41
    arrangements, types of, 36-37
    divided, 38-41
    evaluation, 80-90
    guidelines of American
            Psychological
            Association, 71-72
    joint, 41-44
    split, 38-41

D

Deposition, 121-126

Developmental theory, 23-26, 62-64
    split custody and, 40

Divorce,
    effects of, 1-6
    governmental involvement and, 4
    percentage of in American mar-
           riages, 2

E

Emotionality of parents, 35-36
    and joint custody, 42

Environmental influences on develop-
    ment, 24-26

Evaluation, child custody, 80-90

Expert testimony, 115-136

F

Fact-finder, as opposed to expert
    opinion-giver, 119-120

Family,
    composition of, 2-3
    nontraditional, 3-5
    rights of, 21-23
    structure of, 5-6
    system, evaluating, 86-88

Family systems approach, 9-16, 23-24,
    26, 39, 86
    narrative perspective of, 14

Fee-related problems, 97-100

Financial agreements, 96-97

G

Gender preferences in custody cases,
    18-20

Governmental intrusion in family life,
    grounds for, 22-23

Guardians, role of, 47-49

H

Household composition, census data on,
    2

I

Income statistics and families, 3

Informed consent, 103-104, 111-113

J

Judges,
    discretion of, 29-30
    preference of, 64-65
    as role definers, 74-75

Judicial determinations, 32-33

L

Lawmakers, duty of, 1-2

Least detrimental alternative, 63

Legal discovery, confidentiality and,
    104-108

Legal issues, avoiding testimony about,
    50-51

Legislation, federal, 30-31

Life span developmental objective, 15